Miniature
Flowers in Sugar

Fumi Fukumuro

Acknowledgements

This is a book that was published with the support of so many people who have all contributed in different ways.
My special and wholehearted thanks go to:
Beverley and Rob Dutton who gave me the chance to express the world that I have visualised in this book;
Jenny Stewart and Sarah Richardson who have persevered with my limited command of English to produce this
wonderful book;
Alister Thorpe who has taken luminous and beautiful pictures of my work;
Tombi Peck and Alan Dunn who have given me invaluable support and advice in writing this book.

I hope this book will open up a new world of miniature sugarcrafting to its readers and that they will enjoy the
new challenges and the beauties that are unique to it.

 First published in
December 2007 by B.
Dutton Publishing Limited,
Alfred House, Hones
Business Park, Farnham,
Surrey, GU9 8BB.

Copyright: Fumi Fukumuro 2007

ISBN: 978-1-905113-07-1

Publisher: Beverley Dutton

Editor: Jenny Stewart

Designer: Sarah Richardson

Editorial Assistant: Jenny Royle

Design Assistant: Zena Manicom

Photography: Alister Thorpe

Printed in Slovenia

Foreword

I was absolutely delighted when I was asked if I would like to add a few words into the foreword of this magnificent book.

I have met Fumi on many occasions and have had the fascinating task of judging some of her exquisite designs. Fumi's sugarcraft is as beautiful and delicate looking as she is.

As I made the miniature flowers and miniature arrangements in the book, *Modelling in Cold Porcelain*, written by Alan Dunn and myself (B. Dutton Publishing), I am well aware of the extra dexterity, delicacy and attention to detail required when working in miniature.

This book fully illustrates Fumi's impeccable sugarcraft skills and is a wonderful addition to the passionate cake decorator's library.

Tombi Peck

I first met Fumi several years ago at one of Squires Kitchen's annual exhibitions, so it seems very appropriate that this, her first book, is being published by B. Dutton Publishing (also part of the Squires Group). After this exhibition, Fumi started to attend my classes regularly and through this we became good friends. Her sugarcraft skills and attention to fine, delicate detail was already finely tuned, however she still enjoyed coming to classes for new ideas and inspiration. In every class we shared a mutual admiration for each other's work – she works with such ease and speed and has a natural ability with detailed work.

Fumi knew my work from the various titles that I had already written and I knew almost instantly that it would not be too long before she started to write her own sugarcraft book.

I own many cake decorating and sugarcraft books, however few hold a place on my favourite books shelf – this, Fumi's first book, will be joining my all-time favourites.

I hope you enjoy this book and find Fumi's beautiful work as much of an inspiration as I do.

Alan Dunn

CONTENTS

BASIC TOOLS AND MATERIALS

The tools and materials you use to make your miniature projects play a vital part in creating realistic, delicate pieces. Every project in this book will require most or all of the basic tools and some of the materials listed here, so it is worth having everything to hand before you start. Specific requirements are given at the beginning of each individual project.

Basic Tools

10mm diameter rolling pin
23cm (9") rolling pin
Cellophane piping bags
Ceramic silk veining tool (HP)
Cocktail sticks
Craft knife
Cutters*
Dresden tool (JEM)
Dusting brush: 3mm-width, flat
Fine piping nozzles: nos. 0, 00
Fine, pointed scissors
Fine, pointed tweezers (plain end)
Flexible 'cocktail stick' (CEL)
Floristry tape: various colours*
Floristry wires: various colours and gauges*
High-tack craft glue
Matt and gloss spray varnish (only if using cold porcelain)
Miniature metal ball or bone tools: various sizes
Non-stick board
Paintbrushes: nos. 000005 to 2 (very fine to fine)*
Palette knife (not pictured)
Petal pad
Plain cutting wheel (PME)
Scriber/needle tool (PME)
Wire cutters
Paint palette
Scientific wire*
Stamens*
Veiners*

*See projects for specific colour/size requirements.

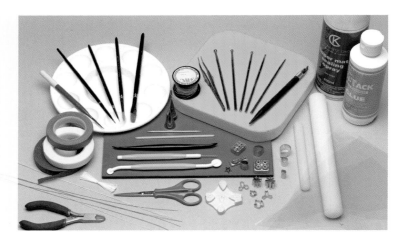

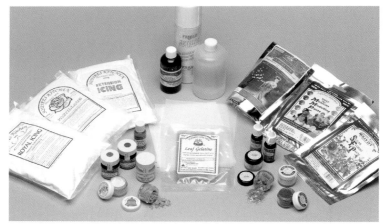

Basic Materials

Clear alcohol (e.g. gin or vodka)
Cornflour duster (not pictured)
Icing sugar duster (not pictured)
SK Edible Glue
SK Confectioners' Glaze
SK Gelatine Sheets
SK Glaze Cleaner (IPA)

SK Instant Mix Sugars: Extension Icing, Pastillage, Royal Icing*
SK Mexican Modelling Paste (MMP)*
SK Professional Dust Food Colours*
SK Professional Liquid Food Colours*
SK Professional Paste Food Colours*
SK Sugar Florist Paste (or cold porcelain)*
White vegetable fat (not pictured)

BASIC TECHNIQUES

Edible Versus Inedible

All of the projects and flowers in this book can be made in either sugar or inedible modelling materials. I generally recommend using edible materials – such as sugarpaste and flower paste (SFP) – for sugarcraft projects, and cold porcelain for ornamental purposes and dolls' houses.

If you are a sugarcrafter or you wish to make one of the miniature cakes as a gift or wedding favour, you can make real miniature cakes (see pages 8 to 9), or simply make each tier from thick sugarpaste cut to size.

IMPORTANT NOTE: Even though edible materials can be used to make all of the miniature flowers and items in the projects, inedible items such as wires, stamens and floristry tape are often used. If a miniature cake is to be consumed, it is vital to ensure that any items that are not approved for food contact do not come into contact with the cake (for example, wires should be inserted into a posy pick, not inserted directly into the cake), and all inedible objects and items that may pose a choking hazard are removed before the cake is eaten. Take extra care to ensure that tiny objects such as wire and stamens, and hidden items, such as cocktail sticks or dried spaghetti used as support, are safely removed.

Alternatively, if you are making a miniature project as an ornament, or for a doll's house or another craft project, you may prefer to use an inedible modelling material such as cold porcelain or silk paste and inedible gouache paints and craft dusts. You can either use styrofoam cake dummies or make each tier from thick paste cut to size (see page 9). If you are working in cold porcelain, remember that it will shrink slightly when drying.

I have used sugarcraft materials where possible throughout the book, although these can be substituted with craft alternatives if required.

Making Miniature Flowers

I have made the flowers in this book to the smallest size at which their natural beauty can be portrayed. Whether you are completely new to sugarcraft or have already made life-size flowers in sugar, it is worth practising a few pieces before embarking on your first project.

The first step to successful miniature flowers is to ensure you have all the correct tools and equipment. Fine wire, fine brushes, fine, pointed tweezers, and good quality miniature tools are all absolutely essential for creating a fine, detailed piece. A full list of basic tools and materials is given opposite.

Otherwise, the basic principles of flower making are the same as life-size flowers. You should use a paste that can be rolled very thinly, i.e. flower paste (SFP) or cold porcelain (depending on the purpose of your project and your own preferences). Always knead the paste well before use and roll out on a board lightly greased with white vegetable fat to prevent it from sticking. When rolling out and cutting flower paste,

use a cornflour duster if necessary to ensure the paste does not become sticky.

As such small quantities of paste are used for each flower, I have used White SFP throughout and added the appropriate SK Professional Paste Food Colours to colour the paste. To save time, you may prefer to buy coloured paste or use any flower paste you already have. Petals and leaves are usually finished with SK Professional Dust Food Colours; always pass dusted pieces through steam to set the colour, otherwise it may rub off.

As I have used edible pastes and colours for the most part, I have used confectioners' glaze to add a shine where needed. Neat glaze will add a high shine, so to reduce the effect, mix it with isopropyl alcohol (sometimes referred to as IPA or glaze cleaner) or a clear spirit such as gin or vodka. Half-strength glaze is made using equal quantities of each. If you are using craft materials, you can use a spray varnish instead.

Remember that flower paste and cold porcelain are both air-drying pastes, so keep any paste that you are not using sealed in an air-tight, food-grade plastic bag.

MAKING A MINIATURE CAKE

There are four methods for making a miniature cake; the context in which you are making the cake will determine which method is best suited to your project. I have used a variety of techniques throughout the projects in this book, but you can adapt each one using any one of the methods below.

Method 1: Baking a miniature fruit cake to size (edible)

If you wish to make a miniature cake as a gift or wedding favour, you will need to source tins of the appropriate size and shape. If you are baking a larger fruit cake, you can put a little of the mixture in the miniature tins for your project. This method is useful for unusually-shaped cakes that are difficult to carve such as the two-tier dome-shaped cake (see Orchid Duet Wedding Cake, pages 92 to 102).

Once you have baked the cake, cover it with marzipan in the same way as for a large cake, as follows:

1. Fill any holes in the cake with small pieces of marzipan.

2. Brush the cake with apricot glaze.

3. Roll out some marzipan and cover the cake. Smooth over the marzipan with the palm of your hand and trim neatly at the base. Allow to firm.

4. Brush the marzipan surface with clear alcohol (e.g. gin or vodka). Roll out some sugarpaste and cover the cake. Smooth the surface and trim to size, as before.

Method 2: Cutting a miniature shape from a larger cake (edible)

If the cakes you are making are a standard shape, you can cut out the tiers from a larger cake using cutters, as follows:

1. Place the cake on its side (a square cake makes this easier) and carefully cut through the middle to make two shallow cakes. The height of the miniature cake will vary, depending on the project and its scale.

2. Cut out the shapes required using deep, metal cutters. Carefully remove the shapes from the cutters.

3. Cover the miniature cakes with marzipan and sugarpaste, as described in Method 1.

Method 3: Making a 'cake' from sugarpaste or cold porcelain (edible or inedible)

You can also make a miniature 'cake' from solid paste (sugarpaste or cold porcelain):

1. Roll out the paste thickly, to the depth of the cake.

2. Cut out the shape of the cake using cutters, as in Method 2. Soften any sharp edges with your fingertip. Allow to firm before stacking or inserting flowers, pillars, etc. (Bear in mind that cold porcelain will shrink slightly when drying.)

Method 4: Cake dummies (inedible)

If you are making a miniature cake project as a keepsake or craft project (e.g. for a doll's house), you may prefer to use styrofoam dummies. These are available in a range of pre-cut shapes from sugarcraft and craft shops, so check that you can obtain the correct sizes and shapes for your project before you begin. Cover the cakes as follows:

1. Brush each dummy one at a time with clear alcohol, edible glue or craft glue.

2. Roll out some sugarpaste and cover the dummy. Smooth and trim the paste as before. Allow the paste to firm before using. (It is difficult to cover a dummy with cold porcelain because it shrinks when drying.)

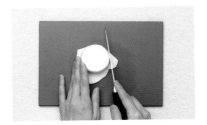

Scale

The size of your miniature projects will depend on the context in which the piece is to be used. Always consider what will be in the background when the piece is on display and how this may affect the overall appearance of the piece. Many dolls' houses are made to a scale of 1:12, so you may need to adjust the sizes for your own requirements.

Roses and Lilies Wedding Cake

THREE-TIER WEDDING CAKE

Materials

Basic materials (see page 6)
100g (3½oz) SK Instant Mix Pastillage
50g (1¾oz) SK Instant Mix Professional
Royal Icing
300g (10½oz) sugarpaste: white

Equipment

Basic tools (see page 6)
Nail file (new)
Oval cutters: set of 9 (A)
Oval template (see page 110)
Peach fabric
Piping nozzle: no. 00
3mm-width ribbon: pale green
10cm (4") round cake card

Miniature Flowers and Foliage

17 roses at various stages (buds, half-open and open flowers)
5 tube roses
6 stems of ivy (16 leaves altogether)
5 stems of eucalyptus leaves
10 calla lilies (see Bridal Bouquet project, pages 31 to 32)

Cakes

1. Roll out the white sugarpaste to a thickness of 1.5cm. Using the oval cutters from the set, with no. 1 as the smallest and no. 9 as the largest, cut out three ovals in sizes 3, 6 and 9. Smooth the cut edge with your finger.

2. Using the no. 2 cutter, cut out a small section from the no. 6 oval. Do the same with the no. 3 cutter from the no. 9 oval. Smooth over the cut edge with your finger.

3. Using a craft knife, make a 5mm-diameter hole towards one edge of the no. 3 oval and the no. 6 oval with the cut-out. This is where the flowers will be positioned. Make holes in the no. 6 and no. 9 ovals with a cocktail stick to support the pillars later (see diagram below).

4. Dust base of the cakes with cornflour, place on a spare board and allow to dry.

Roses and Lilies Wedding Cake Actual Size

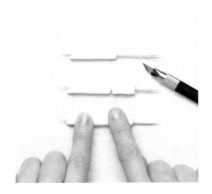

Boards

5. Make up the pastillage following the instructions on the pack. Roll out the paste to a thickness of 3mm and cut out an oval using a no. 4 size cutter and a larger oval using the template and cutting wheel.

6. Place both ovals on a spare board dusted with cornflour and allow to dry overnight. When dry, smooth the cut edge of the ovals with a new nail file.

7. Mix some pastillage with cooled, boiled water to make a paste glue. Place this in a piping bag, snip 1mm off the tip and pipe a line around the edge of the pastillage boards. Secure the 3mm-width ribbon to the board edge and allow to dry.

8. Cut a piece of peach coloured fabric to the size of the cake card and secure it in place using non-toxic craft glue.

Pillar

9. Roll a ball of white pastillage, 1cm in diameter. Insert a cocktail stick through the paste and roll the paste from the centre of the cocktail stick to form a cylinder.

10. Using a craft knife, make a diagonal cut at one end of the paste and a straight cut at the other end. Remove the excess paste and allow to dry overnight. When dry, file the rough edges with a nail file.

11. Using the paste glue, secure the cakes to the boards (the small, oval cake on the small board and the two ovals with cut-outs stacked on the larger board).

12. Secure green ribbon to the edge of the cake boards in the same way as before.

13. Cut the cocktail stick supporting the pillar to the required length, glue the end and insert it into the hole made previously in the middle tier. (Do not add the top tier at this stage.)

14. Place some Professional Royal Icing in a piping bag with a no. 00 nozzle and pipe a line of running beads round the base of each cake.

Side Design

15. Using the same piping bag and nozzle, pipe three dots followed by one dot around the sides of the cakes in a curved pattern. Complete the pattern by adding another three dots to the set of three to make a triangle.

Assembly

16. Push the pillar into position and assemble the tiers, securing the top tier in place with edible glue. Make crescent, 'S' shape and 'V' shape bouquets of miniature roses, tube roses, calla lilies, ivy and eucalyptus and arrange them on the cake.

ROSE

Materials

Basic materials (see page 6)
SK Professional Dust Food Colours:
Edelweiss, Holly/Ivy, Rose, Sunflower
SK Professional Paste Food Colour:
Leaf Green
SK Sugar Florist Paste (SFP): White

Equipment

Basic tools (see page 6)
Calyx cutter: micro (FC)
Craft dust: strawberry
Floristry tape: light green
32-gauge floristry wire: green
30-gauge floristry wire: white
Miniature rose petal cutters or templates (see page 111)
Rose leaf cutter (FC)
Rose leaf veiner: micro (CP)

Bud

1. Cut a 30-gauge white floristry wire into eight equal pieces. Take one piece and make a small hook at the end.

2. Model a small teardrop from White SFP, moisten the wire hook with edible glue and insert it into the wide end of the paste to form the flower centre.

3. Pinch one side of the teardrop between your finger and thumb to flatten the paste. Moisten one side with edible glue and wrap it around the teardrop to make a tight spiral at the top.

Petals

4. Roll out some White SFP and cut out two small petals using the cutter or template. Place them on a petal pad and soften the edges using a miniature metal ball tool.

5. Brush each petal with edible glue and wrap the petals around the flower centre, overlapping the edges. This forms an opening bud.

6. To make a half-open flower, make three more small petals in the same way and wrap them around the bud, ensuring they are positioned in-between each other. Repeat with another three petals to make a more open flower. Curl back the edges of the outer petals.

7. To make an open flower, make five petals using the larger size cutter or template. Soften each one with a ball tool and wrap them around the flower, tucking the edge underneath the previous petal each time. Roll back the edges of these petals to form a natural shape.

Calyx

8. Colour some White SFP with Leaf Green Paste Food Colour. Roll a teardrop shape, then pinch out the paste around the base to make a Mexican hat shape.

9. Using the micro cutter, cut out the calyx shape with the bump of paste in the middle. Make tiny cuts in each sepal using a craft knife.

10. Place the calyx on a petal pad and soften around the edges with a miniature metal ball tool. Use the same tool to cup the calyx, then moisten the centre with edible glue and secure it to the base of the flower.

Colouring

11. Dust the petals with a mixture of Sunflower and Edelweiss Dust Food Colours. Dust from the edge towards the centre with strawberry craft dust, then dust the edges of the petals with Rose Dust Food Colour.

12. Dust the calyx with Holly/Ivy Dust Food Colour, then dust the edges of the calyx with strawberry craft dust.

13. Pass the flower through the steam from a kettle to set the colour, then tape down the stem with $^1/_5$-width floristry tape.

Leaves

14. Cut a 32-gauge green floristry wire into eight equal pieces.

15. Roll out some Leaf Green SFP, leaving a ridge down the centre. Cut out a leaf shape using the cutter. Moisten the end of a piece of floristry wire with edible glue and insert it into the leaf.

16. Vein the leaf using the micro veiner. Place the leaf on a petal pad and soften the edges using a miniature metal ball tool.

17. Dust the edges of the leaf with strawberry craft dust, then dust outwards from the centre of the leaf with Holly/Ivy Dust Food Colour.

18. Tape down the stem with $^1/_5$-width light green floristry tape, then pass through the steam from a kettle to set the colour.

TUBEROSE

Materials

Basic materials (see page 6)
SK Sugar Florist Paste (SFP): White
SK Professional Dust Food Colours:
Edelweiss, Pastel Pink, Sunflower

Equipment

Basic tools (see page 6)
6-pointed petal cutter (CCC)
Floristry tape: light green
35-gauge floristry wire: white
Miniature stamens: white

Flower Centre

1. Cut a 30-gauge white floristry wire into eight equal pieces.

2. Tape together six miniature stamens with ¼-width light green floristry tape. Cut away the excess length from the stamens and tape down to the bottom.

Petals

3. Roll out some White SFP and cut out two 6-pointed blossom shapes. Place them on a petal pad and soften the edge using a miniature metal ball tool. Use the tool to cup each flower in the centre.

4. Make a tiny teardrop from White SFP and pinch out the paste at the thicker end to form a Mexican hat shape. Place the shape on a non-stick board and roll out the base further using a CelStick or cocktail stick.

5. Position the 6-petal cutter over the Mexican hat and cut out the blossom shape. Soften the edges of the blossom and make a hole in the centre using a CelStick or cocktail stick.

6. Moisten the centre of the flower with edible glue and place one of the cupped blossom shapes on top so that the petals sit between the first layer. Repeat with the second blossom shape.

7. Moisten the base of the flower centre with edible glue and thread it down through the centre of the petals. Pinch the paste at the base of the flower to secure it to the wire and remove any excess paste with your fingers.

Bud

8. Cut a 35-gauge white floristry wire into eight equal pieces. Roll a ball of White SFP, dip the end of a piece of wire into edible glue and insert this into the paste.

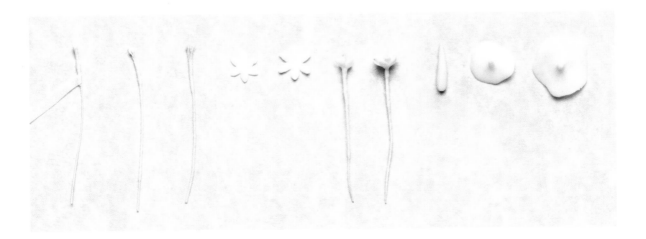

9. Mould the paste with your fingers to form a bud shape, then mark vertical lines down the bud with a craft knife.

Calyx

10. Cut a small leaf shape from light green floristry tape using a pair of fine scissors. Tape one to the base of each flower and bud using ¼-width tape.

Assembly

11. Tape the flowers and buds down the stem, starting at the top with two or three buds, followed by two or three buds and a flower a little further down. Finally, add two or three flowers towards the bottom of the stem.

Colouring

12. Dust the base of the flowers with Leaf Green Dust Food Colour, inside the flowers with a mixture of Sunflower and Edelweiss, and the buds with a mixture of Pastel Pink and Edelweiss. Pass through the steam from a kettle to set the colour.

Calla Lily

For instructions on making the calla lilies, see pages 31 to 32.

IVY

Materials

Basic materials (see page 6)
SK Professional Dust Food Colours:
Forest Green, Holly/Ivy
SK Professional Edible Food Paint:
White
SK Professional Paste Food Colour:
Leaf Green
SK Sugar Florist Paste (SFP): White

Equipment

Basic tools (see page 6)
Craft dust: aubergine
Floristry tape: dark green
35-gauge floristry wire: white
Glass-headed pin
20mm ivy cutter (CCC)
Ivy leaf veiner: micro (CP)

Leaf

1. Cut a piece of 35-gauge floristry wire into eight equal pieces.

2. Colour some White SFP with Leaf Green Paste Food Colour. Roll out the green paste, leaving a ridge down the centre. Cut out the ivy shape using the cutter.

3. Moisten a piece of floristry wire with edible glue and insert it into the ridge of the ivy leaf. Pinch the base of the leaf to secure it to the wire.

4. Vein the leaf in the ivy veiner, then place it on a petal pad and soften around the edge using a miniature metal ball.

5. Dust the leaf from the top downwards with Holly/Ivy Paste Food Colour. Next, dust the leaf from the bottom upwards with Forest Green. Finally, dust the edges with aubergine craft dust.

6. Pass the leaf over the steam from a kettle to set the colour. Dip in ½-strength confectioners' glaze and allow to dry.

7. When dry, paint lines on the leaf using Edible White Paint and a fine paintbrush.

Tendril

8. Cut a ¹⁄₆-width strip of dark green floristry tape, then cut the end into a long point. Twist the pointed end tightly, then tape down a piece of 35-gauge floristry wire.

9. Curl the taped piece of wire around a scriber to make a tiny spiral.

10. Tape the ivy stems using ¹⁄₆-width dark green flower tape. Join the tendrils and leaves together using the same tape.

EUCALYPTUS

Materials

Basic materials (see page 6)
SK Professional Bridal Satin Lustre
Dust Food Colour: White Satin
SK Professional Dust Food Colours:
Blackberry, Edelweiss, Holly/Ivy
SK Professional Paste Food Colour:
Leaf Green
SK Sugar Florist Paste (SFP): White

Equipment

Basic tools (see page 6)
35-gauge floristry wire: white
Craft dust: aubergine
Miniature eucalyptus cutters or
templates (see page 111)

1. Colour some White SFP pale green using a little Leaf Green Paste Food Colour.

2. Roll out the paste on a non-stick board, leaving a ridge down the centre. Cut out the leaf shape using the cutter or template and a cutting wheel.

3. Cut a piece of 35-gauge floristry wire into eight equal pieces. Moisten the top of one piece of wire with edible glue and insert it into the ridge of the leaf. Pinch the base of the leaf to secure it to the wire.

4. Place the leaf on a petal pad and soften around the edge using a miniature metal ball tool.

5. Dust the leaf with a mixture of Blackberry, Edelweiss and Holly/Ivy Dust Food Colours. Brush a little aubergine craft dust on the edge.

6. Cut a piece of white floristry tape to ¼-width, then cut down 5mm from the top in half again so that the top part is $^1/_8$-width. Twist the two narrow pieces of tape at the top.

7. Add a piece of 35-gauge floristry wire below the twisted pieces and tape down the wire.

8. Add two of the smallest leaves and tape down 5mm again. Cut the excess wire off the two leaf stems at this point, then add two medium-sized leaves, tape down 5mm and cut off the excess leaf stems again. Finally, add two of the largest leaves and tape down to the end of the wire (there is no need to trim the stems this time).

9. Dust the stems with Holly/Ivy Dust Food Colour, then pass the leaves over steam to set the colour. Allow to dry.

10. Dust the leaves with White Satin Lustre Dust to give them a sheen.

Assembly

Make a crescent spray for the top tier, an 'S' shape bouquet for the middle tier and a 'V' for the base tier. Start with a rose in the centre to make a focal point, then use tuberoses and calla lilies to outline the shape of each spray. Fill in the spaces with rose buds, eucalyptus and ivy leaves.

Decorative Wedding Cake Plaque

PLAQUE

Materials

Basic materials (see page 6)
30g (1oz) SK Cocoa Butter
150g (¼oz) SK Instant Mix Pastillage
50g (1¾oz) SK Instant Mix Royal Icing
100g (3½oz) SK Mexican Modelling
Paste (MMP): White
SK Professional Dust Food Colours:
Edelweiss, Holly/Ivy, Wedgwood
SK Professional Edible Paints: Brown,
Gold, Yellow
SK Professional Metallic Lustre Dust
Food Colour: Antique Gold
SK Professional Paste Food Colour:
Chestnut
Rice paper

Equipment

Basic tools (see page 6)
12cm and 12.5cm (4¾" and 5") oval
cutters (W)
Nail file (new)
Piping nozzle: no. 00
3mm-width ribbon: gold
Templates: wedding cake, base, stand
(see page 110)

Miniature Flowers and Foliage

8 stems of crassulaceae, various sizes
12 stems of string-of-pearls, various
lengths
8 bunches of viburnum berries,
various sizes
10 poppy seeds
5 pale yellow roses, 2 buds (see Roses
and Lilies Wedding Cake project,
pages 13 to 14)

1. Make up the pastillage following the instructions on the pack. Add a little Wedgwood Dust Food Colour to make a pale blue.

2. Roll out the paste on a non-stick board dusted with cornflour to a thickness of 2mm. Cut out two ovals using the 12cm and 12.5cm cutters, followed by one base shape and two triangle shapes for the stand using the templates.

3. Liberally dust a spare board with cornflour and allow the pastillage pieces to dry hard overnight. When dry, file any sharp edges with a new nail file.

4. Draw the wedding cake shape onto rice paper and trace this onto the plaque using a scriber.

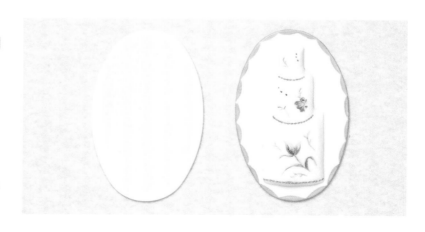

Decorative Wedding Cake Plaque Actual Size

5. Using more rice paper, make the six sections of the wedding cake shape from the template: three pointed oval shapes in graduating sizes for the tops and three curved rectangles for the sides.

6. Colour some White MMP with a little Chestnut Paste Food Colour to make a pale beige tone. Roll out the paste so that the central area is thicker than the edges. The paste should be approximately 5mm thick in the centre and 1mm thick around the edges. Cut out the six pieces using a cutting wheel, ensuring the top pieces are thicker on one edge and the side pieces are thicker in the centre to create the relief effect.

7. Moisten the wedding cake shape on the plaque with edible glue and secure the three-dimensional pieces in place. Roll out some of the beige-coloured MMP to a thickness of 1mm. Cut out the slightly larger wedding cake shape following the dotted line template and cover the wedding cake. Carefully smooth the paste over the shape and allow to dry.

8. Roll out some more beige-coloured MMP to a thickness of 2mm and cut out the base shape using the template. Brush the back with edible glue and secure it towards the back of the small oval.

9. Make up the royal icing following the instructions on the pack. Place some icing in a piping bag with a no. 00 nozzle and pipe a row of dots around the base of the cake and the edge of the base plaque. Add further decoration around the edge of the main plaque and allow to dry.

10. Paint scallops around the edge of the large oval plaque using edible gold paint thickened with Antique Gold Metallic Dust Food Colour. Paint the piped decoration around the edge of the plaque gold.

11. Melt some cocoa butter in a saucer and mix it with various dust colours. Use the cocoa painting technique to add detail on the cake and board.

12. Mix a little of the pale blue pastillage with water to make a thick paste. Use this to glue the two triangular stand pieces to the back of the plaque.

13. Attach gold ribbon to the base board using edible glue.

14. Stand the plaque in position. Wire the flowers into four bouquets. Make holes in the plaque and insert the wires from three of the bouquets through the holes. Secure firmly at the back using the strong pastillage glue made earlier. Place the fourth bouquet on the board.

CRASSULACEAE

Materials

Basic materials (see page 6)
SK Professional Dust Food Colours:
Blackberry, Edelweiss, Holly/Ivy
SK Professional Paste Food Colour:
Sunflower
SK Sugar Florist Paste (SFP): White

Equipment

Basic tools (see page 6)
Craft dust: aubergine
Floristry tape: white
Scientific wire

1. Cut the scientific wire to 3cm lengths.

2. Colour some White SFP pale yellow using a little Sunflower Paste Food Colour. Roll a tiny piece of paste into a teardrop shape, moisten the tip of a length of wire with edible glue and insert it into the pointed end of the teardrop.

3. Press the teardrop between your fingers, then soften the paste using a miniature metal ball tool. Pinch the top between your thumb and finger to make it slightly pointed.

4. Repeat to make several leaves in various sizes.

5. Glue the wired berries together in clusters with high-tack craft glue, then tape the stem with $^1/_6$-width white floristry tape.

6. Dust the leaves with a mixture of Holly/Ivy, Edelweiss and Blackberry Dust Food Colours to make a eucalyptus colour. Dust the edges with aubergine craft dust.

7. Pass through the steam from a kettle to set the colour.

STRING-OF-PEARLS

Materials

Basic materials (see page 6)
SK Sugar Florist Paste (SFP): White
SK Professional Dust Food Colours:
Holly/Ivy, Leaf Green
SK Professional Paste Food Colour:
Sunflower

Equipment

Basic tools (see page 6)
Floristry tape: white
Scientific wire

1. Cut the scientific wire into 3cm lengths.

2. Colour some White SFP pale yellow using a little Sunflower Paste Food Colour. Roll a tiny ball of paste, moisten the tip of a length of wire with edible glue and insert it into the ball of paste.

3. Pinch the top of the paste between your thumb and finger to make a pointed shape. Mark a central vein on the leaf using a plain cutting wheel.

4. Repeat to make several leaves in different sizes.

5. Position the leaves with the smallest ones at the top, increasing the size as you work down. Glue the wires together with high-tack craft glue and tape with $^1/_6$-width white floristry tape. If the stem becomes too wide, cut off one or more of the wires before you tape them together.

6. Colour the leaves with Leaf Green Dust Food Colour. Add some Holly/Ivy Dust Food Colour at the base of each leaf.

7. Pass the leaves through the steam from a kettle to set the colour and dip into ½-strength confectioners' glaze.

VIBURNUM BERRY

Materials

Basic materials (see page 6)
SK Professional Dust Food Colours:
Cyclamen, Hyacinth, Jet Black
SK Professional Paste Food Colours:
Blackberry, Hyacinth
SK Sugar Florist Paste (SFP): White

Equipment

Basic tools (see page 6)
Floristry tape: white
Scientific wire

1. Cut the scientific wire into 5cm lengths.

2. Colour some White SFP with Blackberry and Hyacinth Paste Food Colours to make a dark blue shade. Roll a tiny piece of the coloured paste into a teardrop shape.

3. Moisten the end of a piece of wire with edible glue and insert it into the wide end of the teardrop. Pinch the tip with your fingers to emphasise the point.

4. Repeat this method to make ten to 16 berries per bunch. Tape the berries in bunches using $^{1}/_{6}$-width white floristry tape.

5. Dust the berries with a mixture of Jet Black and Hyacinth Dust Food Colours, then dust the stems with Cyclamen Dust Food Colour.

6. Pass the berries through the steam from a kettle to set the colour and dip into ½-strength confectioners' glaze.

POPPY SEED

Materials

Basic materials (see page 6)
SK Professional Dust Food Colours:
Bulrush, Holly/Ivy, Nasturtium,
Sunflower
SK Professional Paste Food Colour:
Sunflower
SK Sugar Florist Paste (SFP): White

Equipment

Basic tools (see page 6)
Floristry tape: moss green
32-gauge floristry wire: green
8mm rounded 6-petal cutter (CCC)

1. Cut a 32-gauge green floristry wire into 3cm lengths. Make a tiny hook in the end of one piece.

2. Colour some White SFP a pale yellow colour using a little Sunflower Paste Food Colour. Roll a ball of paste measuring 2mm and form this into a teardrop shape. Moisten the wire hook with edible glue and thread the wire down through the wide end of the teardrop. Pull the wire down until the hook is embedded in the paste.

3. Re-mould the paste into a teardrop with your fingers and mark six to eight lines down the sides of the paste using the back of a craft knife.

4. Roll out some pale yellow-coloured SFP and cut out a rounded 6-petal blossom using the cutter. Using angled tweezers, pinch a line down the centre of each petal. Trim the tip off each petal using a pair of fine scissors.

5. Turn over the blossom shape and brush the centre with edible glue. Place it centrally on top of the teardrop. Add a tiny ball of paste at the base of the teardrop for the seedpod.

6. Dust the head (top part) with a mixture of Nasturtium and Sunflower Dust Food Colours and the seed (teardrop shape) with Holly/Ivy. Dilute some Bulrush Dust Food Colour with a little clear alcohol and paint the lines on the seed head.

7. Pass the poppy seed through the steam from a kettle and allow to dry. Dip into ½-strength confectioners' glaze.

Rose

For instructions on making the roses, see pages 13 to 14. You will need to make five pale yellow roses and two buds for the bouquets.

Assembly

1. Wire together three round bouquets for the cake tiers, using the roses and crassulaceae in the centre and the viburnum berries and poppy seeds towards the edges. Add stems of string-of-pearls trailing from the top and bottom of each one. Keep the wires long enough to insert through the plaque.

2. Make a fourth, smaller bouquet for the board and add a short stem of string-of-pearls at the top. Cut the wires short and place this to one side of the cake on the board.

Bridal Bouquet

WEDDING DRESS

Materials

Basic materials (see page 6)
Cake sparkles: pink (W)
50g (1¾oz) SK Instant Mix Pastillage
50g (1¾oz) SK Instant Mix Professional
Royal Icing
300g (10½oz) SK Mexican Modelling
Paste (MMP): White
SK Professional Dust Food Colours:
Pastel Pink, Sunflower, Vine
SK Professional Metallic Lustre Dust
Food Colour: Antique Gold
SK Professional Paste Food Colour:
Chestnut
300g (10½oz) silk paste (CEL) (or use SK
Mexican Modelling Paste if preferred)
200g (7oz) sugarpaste: white
Waffle paper or rice paper

Equipment

Basic tools (see page 6)
7mm, 10mm and 16mm (¹/₄", ³/₈" and
⁵/₈") circle cutters
Dowelling rod (optional)
Dress templates (see page 111)
Heart shape punch cutter
15cm (6") petal shape cake card
Piping nozzle: no. 00
3mm-width ribbon: white
Textured rolling pin: bubbles (JEM)
Waffle paper or rice paper
Woman body mould (PME)

Miniature Flowers and Foliage

3 Casablanca lilies
3 calla lilies
8 hypericum berries
3 alstroemeria flowers, 4 buds, 3 leaves

Body

1. Colour some White MMP with a little Chestnut Paste Food Colour to make a flesh colour.

2. Dust the body mould with cornflour to prevent the paste from sticking. Roll the MMP into a sausage shape and narrow at the neck and waist. Push the paste into the mould and carefully turn it out onto the work surface.

3. Trim away any excess paste from around the body shape using a pair of fine scissors. Smooth over any rough edges using a bone tool, then make stitch marks down the body using a quilting wheel. To give the dress extra stability, you can insert a dowelling rod into the base of the body if required. Allow to dry hard, preferably for a week.

4. Model the skirt shape from the Chestnut-coloured paste. If you are using a dowel, push it into the top of the skirt to make a hole and remove. Allow to dry, again for a week if possible.

5. Join the body and skirt together using edible glue.

6. Roll out some white silk paste or MMP to a thickness of 5mm and cut out a small circle using the 7mm cutter. Secure this to the top of the neck with edible glue. Model a small teardrop of White SFP and secure this on top of the circle.

7. Dilute some Antique Gold Lustre Dust with clear alcohol and paint the circle and teardrop.

Bridal Bouquet Actual Size

Dress

8. Roll out some silk paste or MMP and cut out a rectangle measuring 11cm x 30cm (4¼" x 12") for the skirt. Make several tucks along one side and secure it in place on the body with edible glue, ensuring the join is at the back.

9. Cut out the bodice from silk paste and secure it in place on the body.

10. Cut out two pieces for the sleeves using the template and create a draped effect using a cocktail stick. Gather the paste at each end and attach to the dress using edible glue.

11. Make the pieces required for the ribbons, form them into a bow and attach to the back of the dress.

12. Place some royal icing in a piping bag with a no. 00 nozzle and pipe a filigree pattern at the bottom of the skirt and on the bodice. Add a pearl necklace around the neck.

Board

13. Colour the sugarpaste pale yellow using a little Sunflower Paste Food Colour. Dampen the cake card and cover it with the paste, then roll over the surface with a textured rolling pin. Trim the edge neatly and secure the ribbon in place.

14. Using waffle paper or rice paper, cut out several heart shapes using a punch cutter and dust them with Pastel Pink, Sunflower and Vine Dust Food Colours. Place them around the edge of the covered board.

Flower Stand

15. Roll out a sausage of pastillage, to a thickness of 5mm. Cut out two circles measuring 10mm and 16mm for the base. Roll the remaining pastillage into a column 6cm long, ensuring it is completely straight. Mark a straight line down the paste using a cutting wheel, then make a hole inside the column to hold the flowers later.

16. Cut out a short strip of paste and bend it round into a circle to fit on top of the stand. Allow all the stand pieces to dry hard.

17. Assemble the flower stand using edible to hold the pieces secure. Using a no. 00 piping nozzle, pipe a row of beads around the top and base of the stand to hide the joins.

18. Place the dress towards the back of the board and the flower stand at the front. Make a cascading bouquet and place this in the stand.

CALLA LILY

Materials

Basic materials (see page 6)
SK Professional Dust Food Colours: Cyclamen, Forest Green, Holly/Ivy, Pastel Pink, Sunflower, Vine
SK Professional Edible Food Paint: White
SK Professional Paste Food Colours: Holly/Ivy, Sunflower
SK Professional Pollen Style Dust Food Colour: Pale Yellow
SK Sugar Florist Paste (SFP): White

Equipment

Basic tools (see page 6)
Craft dust: aubergine
Floristry tape: light green
30-gauge floristry wire: white
Miniature calla lily cutter or template (see page 111)
Miniature calla lily leaf cutter or template (see page 111)
Paintbrush: no. 00000

Flower

1. Cut a piece of 30-gauge white floristry wire into quarters. Make a small hook in the end of one of the pieces.

2. Colour some White SFP yellow using Sunflower Paste Food Colour. Roll a small sausage of paste, moisten the wire hook with edible glue and insert it into the paste.

3. Tape down the wire with ⅓-width light green floristry tape.

Dip the sausage of paste into edible glue and then into Pale Yellow Pollen Dust to cover it.

4. Roll out some White SFP and cut out the petal shape using the cutter or template. Texture using a silk veining tool, then place on a petal pad and soften around the edge using a miniature metal ball tool.

5. Using a 3mm flat brush, dust inside the petal with aubergine craft dust.

6. Brush edible glue on the base of the petal using a fine paintbrush and wrap it around the flower centre. Gently curl back the edge of the petal to give movement.

7. Dust the flower with Vine, Sunflower, Pastel Pink and Cyclamen Dust Food Colours. Pass through the steam from a kettle to set the colour.

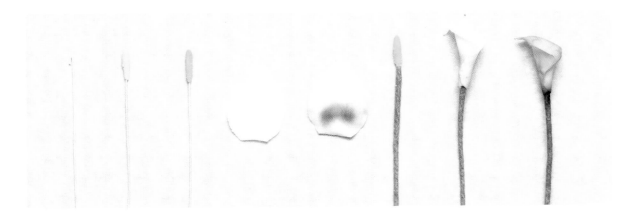

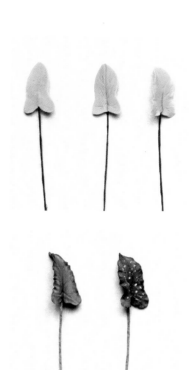

Leaves

8. Colour some SFP with Holly/Ivy Paste Food Colour. Roll out the paste, leaving a ridge in the centre, and cut out the leaf shape using the cutter or template.

9. Moisten a piece of 30-gauge floristry wire with edible glue and insert it into the leaf.

10. Place on a petal pad and vein using the pointed end of a Dresden tool. Soften around the edge of the leaf with a miniature metal ball tool.

11. Dust the leaf with Forest Green and Holly/Ivy Dust Food Colours, then pass over the steam from a kettle to set the colour. Brush with ½-strength confectioners' glaze and allow to dry.

12. Using a no. 00000 paintbrush and White Edible Food Paint, paint tiny spots onto the leaf and allow to dry.

CASABLANCA LILY

Materials

Basic materials (see page 6)
SK Professional Dust Food Colours:
Edelweiss, Holly/Ivy, Leaf Green, Vine
SK Professional Paste Food Colour:
Leaf Green
SK Sugar Florist Paste (SFP): White

Equipment

Basic tools (see page 6)
Craft dust: aubergine
Floristry tape: light green
35-gauge floristry wire: white
Miniature Casablanca lily cutters or
templates (see page 111)
Miniature Casablanca lily leaf cutter or
template (see page 111)
Miniature stamens: white

Pistil

1. Cut a 35-gauge white floristry wire into eight equal pieces. Roll a tiny ball of White SFP and insert a moistened piece of wire.

2. Mould the paste into a 'T' shape 5mm long and cut the top into three sections to form the pistil shape.

3. Roll another tiny piece of White SFP and thread this up the wire to meet the bottom of the pistil. Secure in place with edible glue.

Stamens

4. Take six miniature, fine stamens and cut off the heads.

5. Roll a tiny ball of White SFP, moisten the end of a stamen and insert the stamen into the paste. Mould the paste into an elongated, curved shape. Repeat to make six stamens for each flower.

6. Tape the pistil and stamens together using ⅓-width light green floristry tape.

7. Dust the top of the pistil with aubergine craft dust and the stamens with Vine Dust Food Colour.

Petals

8. Roll out some White SFP, leaving a ridge down the centre. Cut out the wide petal shape using the cutter or template.

9. Cut a 35-gauge white floristry wire into eight equal pieces. Moisten the end of one of the pieces and insert it into the leaf.

10. Mark a central vein on the leaf using a Dresden tool, then soften around the edge using a miniature metal ball tool. Pinch the petal and curl it backwards, then snip spikes into the surface of the petal using fine, curved scissors.

11. Repeat to make three wide petals for each flower.

12. Roll out some White SFP, leaving a ridge down the centre, and cut out the narrow petal shape. Insert a moistened piece of 35-gauge white floristry wire into the petal.

13. Mark a central vein with the Dresden tool, then pinch and curl back the petal, as before. Make three for each flower.

14. Dust the top and base of each leaf with a mixture of Leaf Green and Edelweiss Dust Food Colours.

15. Tape the three wide petals to the centre with ⅓-width light green floristry tape, then add the narrow petals in-between and beneath them.

16. Pass the flower through the steam from a kettle to set the colour.

Bud

17. Roll a sausage of White SFP and insert a moistened 35-gauge white floristry wire.

18. Mark three vertical lines down the paste using a craft knife and pinch the edges with your fingers to accentuate the three sections.

19. Tape down the wire using ⅕-width light green floristry tape.

20. Dust the top and base of the bud with a mixture of Vine and Edelweiss Dust Food Colours and pass through the steam from a kettle to set the colour.

Leaves

21. Colour some White SFP pale green using a little Leaf Green Paste Food Colour. Roll out the paste, leaving a ridge down the centre, and cut out the leaf using the cutter or template.

22. Moisten the end of a piece of 35-gauge white floristry wire and insert this into the leaf. Mark a few veins on the leaf using a plain cutting wheel, then soften around the edges with a miniature metal ball tool.

23. Dust the leaf with a mixture of Leaf Green and Holly/Ivy Dust Food Colours. Pass through the steam from a kettle to set the colour and allow to dry.

24. Dip the leaf into ½-strength confectioners' glaze and allow to dry.

HYPERICUM BERRY

Materials

Basic materials (see page 6)
SK Professional Dust Food Colours:
Bulrush, Fuchsia, Leaf Green,
Nasturtium
SK Professional Paste Food Colours:
Leaf Green, Sunflower
SK Sugar Florist Paste (SFP): White

Equipment

Basic tools (see page 6)
4mm 5-petal blossom cutter (CCC)
Floristry tape: light green
32-gauge floristry wire: green
Miniature stamens: white

Berry

1. Cut a 32-gauge green floristry
    wire into eight equal pieces.
    Make a small hook at the end of
    each piece.

2. Cut off the heads of a miniature
    stamen and paint it with a
    mixture of Bulrush Dust Food
    Colour and clear alcohol. Cut the
    stamen into 2mm lengths.

3. Colour a small amount of White
    SFP pale yellow using Sunflower
    Paste Food Colour. Roll a tiny
    ball of this paste and insert a
    moistened 32-gauge green
    floristry wire. Re-shape the paste
    to form a teardrop shape with
    the point at the top.

4. Make a hole in the tip of the
    teardrop using a scriber. Pick up
    one of the 2mm brown stamens
    with tweezers and insert it into
    the hole.

5. Mark three lines down the sides
    of the teardrop using a craft knife.

Calyx

6. Colour some White SFP with
    a little Leaf Green Paste Food
    Colour to make a pale green
    tone. Roll out the paste on a
    non-stick board and cut out a
    5-petal blossom shape using the
    micro cutter.

7. Using a craft knife,
    make cuts between
    the petals to separate
    them further. Place the
    blossom on a petal pad and
    soften around the edges with a
    miniature metal ball tool. Cup
    the blossom by pushing the tool
    into the centre.

8. Turn the calyx over so that the
    sepals are pointing downwards.
    Brush edible glue in the centre
    and thread it up the wire to the
    base of the berry.

Colouring

9. Dust the top of the berry with
    Fuchsia Dust Food Colour, the
    middle with Nasturtium and the
    bottom with Leaf Green. Colour
    the calyx with Leaf Green, then
    brush the edges with Fuchsia.
    Pass through the steam from
    a kettle to set the colour and
    allow to dry.

10. Dip the berry into ½-strength
    confectioners' glaze and allow
    to dry.

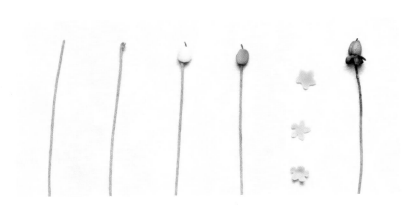

ALSTROEMERIA

Materials

Basic materials (see page 6)
SK Professional Dust Food Colours:
Holly/Ivy, Leaf Green, Marigold, Pastel
Pink, Thrift
SK Professional Paste Food Colours:
Cyclamen, Leaf Green
SK Sugar Florist Paste (SFP): White

Equipment

Basic tools (see page 6)
Floristry tape: light green
32-gauge floristry wire: green
35-gauge floristry wire: white
Miniature stamens: white
Paintbrush: no. 00000

Flower Centre

1. Cut a 35-gauge white floristry wire
    into eight equal pieces. Make a
    small hook at the end of one piece.

2. Roll a 3mm ball of White SFP and
    mould it into a teardrop shape.
    Hollow out the wide end using a
    cocktail stick.

Petals

3. Using a pair of fine, pointed
    scissors, snip the flower centre
    at the wide end into three equal
    sections and fold each part back
    to open up the flower. Snip each
    of the three parts in two, dividing
    them roughly into $\frac{1}{3}$ and $\frac{2}{3}$
    sections.

4. Pinch each of the wide and
    narrow sections from the sides
    and then from the top and
    bottom to create six pointed
    petals.

5. Using a small wheel tool, mark
    a line down the centre of each
    petal. Turn the flower over, place
    it on a petal pad and soften the
    petals from the back using a
    miniature metal ball tool.

6. Using the pointed end of a
    Dresden tool, make several
    notches along the top half of
    the petal edges.

7. Moisten the hooked piece of
    wire with edible glue and thread
    the flower up to the hook from
    the bottom. Pinch the base of

the flower and trim away any
excess paste.

8. Use fine, smooth-edged
    tweezers to pinch the tip of
    each petal backwards. Using
    your fingers, push two of the
    narrow petals together to
    overlap the wide petal between
    them. Bend the other narrow
    petal back on itself.

Stamens

9. Cut the heads off the miniature
    stamens, then paint with Thrift
    and Pastel Pink Dust Food
    Colour mixed with clear alcohol.
    Cut the stamen into 3mm
    lengths.

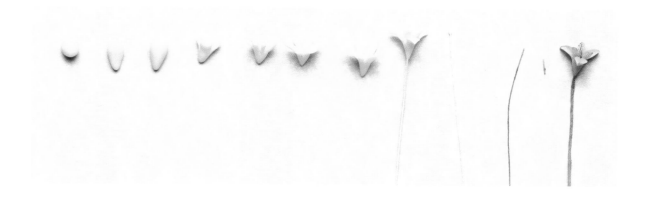

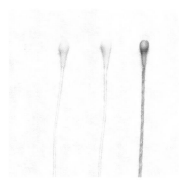

10. Moisten the flower centre with edible glue and use tweezers to push the stamens into place. Bend them slightly so that they curve upwards.

Colouring

11. Brush the tips and undersides of the petals with Leaf Green Dust Food Colour. Dust the top area of the petals with Marigold and the base with a mixture of Thrift and Pastel Pink Dust Food Colours.

12. Dilute a little Cyclamen Liquid Food Colour with clear alcohol. Using a no. 00000 paintbrush, paint dots and lines onto the narrow petals.

13. Tape the stem with ¹⁄₃-width light green floristry tape and pass through the steam from a kettle to set the colour.

Bud

14. Make a hook in the end of a piece of 35-gauge white floristry wire. Roll a tiny ball of White SFP into a teardrop shape, moisten the wire hook with edible glue and insert it into the paste.

15. Divide the bud into three sections using a cutting wheel, then pinch each section to emphasise the shape.

16. Dust the buds with Leaf Green Dust Food Colour, then add the Thrift and Pastel Pink mixture used on the petals.

17. Tape down the stem with ¹⁄₃-width light green floristry tape and pass the bud through steam to set the colour.

Leaves

18. Cut a 32-gauge green floristry wire into eight equal pieces.

19. Colour some White SFP with Leaf Green Paste Food Colour. Roll out the paste, leaving a ridge down the centre. Cut out the leaf shape freehand using a cutting wheel and insert a moistened piece of wire.

20. Mark veins from the base of the petal to the tip using a cutting wheel. Twist the leaf to give movement.

21. Dust with a mixture of Leaf Green and Holly/Ivy Dust Food Colours, then pass through steam to set the colour.

Assembly

Tape three Casablanca lilies together in a triangle to form the focal point of the arrangement. Add three calla lilies, one at the top and two at the bottom to create the line of the bouquet. Fill in the spaces between the lilies with the alstroemeria flowers, buds and leaves and the hypericum berries.

An English Country Garden

GARDEN TABLE AND CHAIR

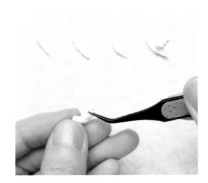

Materials

Basic materials (see page 6)
Cake sparkles: blue (W)
100g (3½oz) caster sugar
SK Liquid Glucose
200g (7oz) SK Instant Mix Pastillage
50g (1¾oz) SK Instant Mix Royal Icing
SK Professional Paste Food Colours:
Hyacinth, Leaf Green
100g (3½oz) sugarpaste: white

Equipment

Angle-poise lamp
Basic tools (see page 6)
3cm, 4cm and 6.5cm (1⅛", 1½" and
2½" circle cutters
Fine cotton net (tulle)
Glass chopping board
35mm and 16cm (1⅜" and 6¼") oval
cutters
Nail file (new)
Piping nozzle: no. 00
3mm-width ribbon: blue
Saucepan
Table and chair templates (see page
110)
Tracing paper
Wax paper

Table and Chair

1. Make up the royal icing and pastillage, following the instructions on the pack.

2. Roll out the pastillage to a thickness of 3mm. Cut out a hexagon for the tabletop using the template and a small knife. Cut out a circle from the centre of the hexagon using a 6.5cm diameter cutter. Leave to dry overnight on a spare board dusted with cornflour.

3. Roll out some pastillage, this time to a thickness of 6mm. Cut out four legs using the template and a small knife, then bend the end of each one slightly to form a curve. Allow to dry overnight.

4. Roll out some more pastillage to a thickness of 3mm. Cut out a 4cm circle for the seat using either a round cutter or the template. Cut out a 3cm circle from the centre, again using a cutter or template. Allow to dry overnight.

5. Roll some pastillage into a long, thin sausage shape, approximately 3mm wide. Cut out a piece for the back of the chair and bend it into an inverted 'U' shape.

6. Make four chair legs, following the template. Allow to dry overnight.

7. Place 100g of caster sugar and 50ml of water into a saucepan and heat gently to melt the sugar. Add a teaspoon of liquid glucose, mix well and remove from the heat.

8. Dip a piece of fine cotton net into the sugar solution and leave for five minutes.

An English Country Garden Actual Size

9. Carefully remove the net from the solution, allow the excess liquid to drip off and lay it flat on a glass chopping board. Wipe off any remaining solution with kitchen paper and place under an angle-poise lamp to dry.

10. When dry, cut out the tabletop, chair seat and chair back using the dotted line templates.

11. File away any sharp edges on the pastillage pieces using a new nail file. Prepare some strong sugar glue by mixing some pastillage powder with edible glue or cooled, boiled water to make a paste. Place this in a piping bag and snip off the tip.

12. Glue the pastillage pieces together in turn using the sugar glue. Start by securing the large, round net piece to the tabletop, then glue the table legs to the table. Glue the chair seat and legs in the same way. Finally, add the last piece of net to the back of the chair and secure this to the seat.

13. Place some royal icing in a piping bag with a no. 00 nozzle. Pipe decorative patterns around the edges of the pieces and the line work on the back of the chair.

Plaque

14. Roll out some pastillage fairly thinly and cut out a 35mm oval using a cutter. Make scallops and holes around the edge using a cocktail stick.

15. Colour a small amount of royal icing with Hyacinth Paste Food Colour, place it in a piping bag with a no. 00 nozzle and pipe 'Welcome', or an inscription of your choice.

16. Decorate the plaque with a small spray of strawberries.

Board

17. Colour some sugarpaste with Hyacinth and Leaf Green Paste Food Colours to make an aquamarine colour. Roll out the paste, cover the oval board and trim to size.

18. Secure blue ribbon around the edge of the board, then secure the table and chair in place using the sugar glue.

19. To finish, sprinkle blue cake sparkles on the board.

TWO-TIER MINIATURE WEDDING CAKE

Materials

Basic materials (see page 6)
SK Instant Mix Royal Icing
SK Mexican Modelling Paste (MMP): White
SK Professional Edible Food Paint: White
SK Professional Paste Food Colours: Hyacinth, Leaf Green
300g (10½oz) sugarpaste: white

Equipment

Basic tools (see page 6)
4cm and 5cm (1½" and 2") circle cutters
2cm and 2.5cm x 1.5cm height (¾" and 1" x ⅝" height) round styrofoam cake dummies
Miniature straight frill cutters or templates (see page 110)

Miniature Flowers and Foliage

16 strawberries (green and red), 4 flowers, 6 leaves
6 carnations
3 bunches of grapes, 5 leaves

1. Make three holes in each of the cake dummies using a cocktail stick: this will be where the pillars are positioned, so make the holes in the top of the base tier and underneath the top tier.

2. Brush the dummies with edible glue. Roll out the white sugarpaste to a thickness of 5mm and cover both cake dummies. Smooth the surface and trim neatly at the base.

3. Cut three cocktail sticks to the required length for the pillars (allowing for the ends to be inserted into the cakes) and paint each piece with White Edible Food Paint. Allow to dry. When dry, insert the pillars into the base tier.

4. Colour some White MMP with Hyacinth and Leaf Green Paste Food Colours to make a pale aqua tone. Roll out the paste and cut out a circle using a 5cm cutter. Make a scalloped edge using a cocktail stick, then make a hole in each scallop for added decoration. Allow to dry.

5. Make another decorative circle in the same way using White MMP and a 4cm circle cutter. Secure this on top of the larger circle with edible glue, then secure the cake on top. Secure the top tier to the pillars using edible glue.

6. Roll out the remaining aqua-coloured MMP and cut out a strip to go around the base of the cakes using the straight frill lace cutter. (Alternatively, you could use a ribbon cutter and cut a decorative edge using a miniature calyx cutter.) Secure around the cakes with edible glue and pipe a few dots of royal icing around each one to decorate.

7. Make two teardrop-shaped corsage arrangements of grapes, carnations and strawberries and secure them on the top and bottom tiers of the wedding cake.

BLUEBIRDS

Materials

Basic materials (see page 6)
SK Instant Mix Professional Royal Icing
SK Modelling Paste (MMP): White
SK Professional Paste Food Colours:
Bulrush, Hyacinth

Equipment

Basic tools (see page 6)
Piping nozzle: no. 1
Wax paper
Wing templates (see page 110)

1. Make up some royal icing, following the instructions on the pack. Colour the icing with Hyacinth Paste Food Colour.

2. Trace the template onto paper and place a sheet of wax paper over the top. Place some of the blue icing in a piping bag with a no. 1 nozzle and pipe the wings onto the wax paper. Repeat to make two sets of wings (plus spares in case of breakages). Allow to dry.

3. Roll a 3mm diameter ball of White MMP and form this into a teardrop shape. Mark the head at the wide end using a Dresden tool, then pinch a tiny beak between your finger and thumb. Curve the pointed end to form the body shape.

4. Mark feathers and eyes using a Dresden tool. Pinch the tail flat and make several small cuts using fine, pointed scissors. Make two cuts in the back using a craft knife.

5. Remove the wings from the wax paper and insert them into the holes in the back of the bird. Secure them in place with edible glue.

6. Repeat to make a second bird in the same way. Paint the bodies with Hyacinth Paste Food Colour diluted with clear alcohol, then paint the eyes and beak with diluted Bulrush Paste Food Colour.

7. Using the strong sugar glue made earlier, secure the bluebirds to the table and chair.

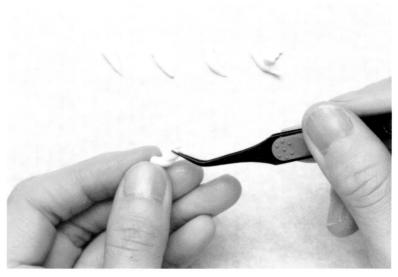

STRAWBERRY

Materials

Basic materials (see page 6)
SK Instant Mix Royal Icing
SK Professional Dust Food Colours:
Holly/Ivy, Leaf Green, Rose
SK Professional Liquid Food Colour:
Holly/Ivy
SK Professional Paste Food Colours:
Leaf Green, Rose, Sunflower
SK Sugar Florist Paste (SFP): White

Equipment

Basic tools (see page 6)
4mm 5-petal blossom cutter (CCC)
Floristry tape: light green
32-gauge floristry wire: green
Miniature strawberry leaf cutters or templates
(see page 111)
Miniature strawberry leaf (or rose leaf) veiner
(CP)
Paintbrush: no. 00
Piping nozzle: no. 00
Small, round, dull-headed stamens: white

Fruit

1. Cut a 32-gauge green floristry wire into eight equal pieces. Make a small hook in the end of one piece. Moisten the hook with edible glue.

2. Colour a small amount of White SFP with Rose or Sunflower Paste Food Colour. Roll a tiny ball of the yellow paste into a teardrop shape and insert the moistened wire into the wide end. Make holes all over the surface of the paste using a scriber.

3. Dust the strawberry with Rose and Holly/Ivy Dust Food Colours, or with Leaf Green for a younger fruit. Pass through the steam from a kettle to set the colour.

4. Dip the strawberry into ½-strength confectioners' glaze and allow to dry.

Flowers

5. Cut the stamens in half and dust the tips with Holly/Ivy Dust Food Colour.

6. Roll out some White SFP and cut out a flower shape using the 4mm blossom cutter. Cut between each of the petals using fine scissors to separate the petals.

7. Place the blossom on a petal pad, then soften and cup the petals using a miniature metal ball tool.

8. Using a no. 00 paintbrush, brush some edible glue on the centre of the blossom and thread it up

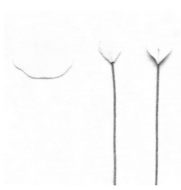

the wire to the stamen. Pinch the petals back to give the required shape.

9.   Pass the flower through the steam from a kettle to set the colour on the stamen.

Calyx

10.   Colour a small amount of royal icing with Holly/Ivy Liquid Food Colour and place in a piping bag with a no. 00 piping nozzle. Pipe a calyx onto the base of each strawberry and each flower and allow to dry.

11.   When dry, dust each calyx with a mixture of Holly/Ivy and Leaf Green Dust Food Colours. Dust the base of the flower with Holly/Ivy Dust Food Colour.

Leaves

12.   Colour some White SFP with Holly/Ivy Paste Food Colour. Roll out the paste on a non-stick board, leaving a ridge down the centre. Cut out a leaf using the cutter or template. Repeat to make three leaves in varying sizes and insert a moistened wire into the base of each one.

13.   Vein each leaf using the miniature strawberry leaf or rose leaf veiner. Place on a petal pad and soften around the edges from the base to the tip using a miniature metal ball tool. Pinch the sides back to give movement.

14.   Dust the leaves with Rose and Holly/Ivy Dust Food Colours, then pass through the steam from a kettle to set the colour.

15.   Dip the leaves into ½-strength confectioners' glaze and allow to dry.

16.   Tape the three leaves together with one at the top and the other two opposite each other on either side using ¹/₅-width light green floristry tape.

CARNATION

Materials

Basic materials (see page 6)
SK Professional Dust Food Colours:
Antique White, Berberis, Edelweiss,
Holly/Ivy
SK Professional Paste Food Colour:
Leaf Green
SK Sugar Florist Paste (SFP): White

Equipment

Basic tools (see page 6)
5-pointed calyx cutter: micro (CEL)
Carnation cutter: small (KB)
Floristry tape: light green
33-gauge floristry wire: white

Petals

1. Cut a 33-gauge white wire into eight equal pieces. Make a tiny hook at one end, moisten with edible glue and cover with a small ball of White SFP.

2. Roll out some White SFP and cut out a flower shape using the carnation cutter. Cut in-between each of the petals using fine, pointed scissors to separate the petals.

3. Rub a little white vegetable fat onto the side of your forefinger, rest the paste on top and frill each petal using a cocktail stick or needle frilling tool.

4. Brush some edible glue in the centre of the flower shape using a fine paintbrush and thread it up the wire to the ball of paste. Fold the flower shape in half, then fold each edge towards the centre, one in front and one behind, to make an 'S' shape. Pinch the base to narrow the paste and secure it firmly to the wire. This is a half-open flower.

5. To make an open flower, follow steps 1 to 4 to the half-open flower stage. Make another blossom shape in the same way as before, thread this up the wire and push it through the narrow base

of the flower to the top. Carefully gather and fold the paste to make a realistic flower shape.

Calyx

6. Colour some White SFP with a little Leaf Green Paste Food Colour to make pale green. Roll out the paste on a non-stick board and cut out a calyx shape using the micro cutter.

7. Place the calyx onto a petal pad and soften around the edge using a miniature metal ball tool. Brush a little edible glue in the centre of the calyx and thread it

up the wire, then wrap it around the base of the flower.

8. Turn the flower upside down and make five cuts around the base of the calyx using fine, pointed scissors.

Colouring

9. Using a no. 2 paintbrush, dust the flower with Antique White Pastel Dust Food Colour, then over-dust with a mixture of Berberis and Edelweiss Dust Food Colours. Dust the calyx with Holly/Ivy.

10. Pass the flower through the steam from a kettle to set the colour.

Leaves

11. Cut a piece of floristry tape into a long triangle to form a leaf shape. Using ¹/₅-width floristry tape, tape down the stem of the flower, adding in two or three leaves at different levels. Curve the leaves with your fingers.

GRAPE VINE

Materials

Basic materials (see page 6)
SK Professional Dust Food Colours: Holly/Ivy, Leaf Green, Vine
SK Professional Paste Food Colour: Leaf Green
SK Sugar Florist Paste (SFP): White

Equipment

Basic tools (see page 6)
Craft dust: aubergine
Floristry tape: light green
32-gauge floristry wire: light green
Glass-headed pin
Leaf veiner: micro (CP)
Paintbrushes: nos. 00, 1
Vine leaf cutter: midi (KB)

Grapes

1. Cut a 32-gauge green floristry wire into eight equal pieces. Make a small hook in one end.

2. Colour a small amount of White SFP with Vine Paste Food Colour. Roll a small teardrop shape, moisten the hooked wire with edible glue and insert it into the pointed end of the teardrop.

3. Make another, longer teardrop of paste and thread this up the wire so that both pointed ends meet. Bend the wire to form a slight curve.

4. Make several teardrops of paste and secure them on top of the long teardrop using edible glue and a no. 00 paintbrush. Working from the end down the wire, build up the shape to form a bunch of grapes.

5. Dust the grapes with a mixture of Vine and Leaf Green Dust Food Colours using a no. 1 paintbrush. Add a little Leaf Green Dust mixed with aubergine to areas that are slightly darker.

6. Pass through the steam from a kettle, allow to dry, then dip into ½-strength confectioners' glaze.

Tendril

7. Take a ⅛ piece of light green floristry wire wind it around a pin to form a tiny spiral.

Leaves

8. Roll out some Leaf Green-coloured SFP, leaving a ridge down the centre. Cut out a leaf using the grape vine leaf cutter. Moisten the end of a piece of 32-gauge wire with edible glue and insert it into the ridge.

9. Vein the leaf in a micro ivy veiner, then place on a petal pad and soften around the edges using a miniature metal ball tool. Pinch the leaf from the back to give it movement.

10. Dust the leaf with Vine and Holly/Ivy Dust Food Colours. Mix some Holly/Ivy and aubergine dusts and lightly over-dust the leaf. Pass through the steam from a kettle to set the colour.

11. Dip the leaf into ½-strength confectioners' glaze and allow to dry.

Assembly

1. To make the spray for the base tier, tape a bunch of grapes, one tendril and one leaf together. Repeat with a second, slightly smaller bunch of grapes. Tape three carnations together with ⅕-width light green floristry tape, then tape the grapes and carnations together. Add seven strawberries, two flowers and three leaves between the carnations and grapes.

2. Repeat to make a second spray for the top tier, using one bunch of grapes with a leaf and tendril, two extra grape leaves, three carnations, six strawberries and one flower. Place each spray into the hole in each cake.

3. Tape three strawberries and three leaves around a strawberry flower. Secure this to the top of the plaque using royal icing or edible glue.

Ornamental Fan Wedding Cake

FAN AND FOUR-TIER MINIATURE WEDDING CAKE

Materials

Basic materials (see page 6)
100g (3½oz) SK Instant Mix Pastillage
50g (1¾oz) SK Instant Mix Royal
Icing
SK Professional Edible Paints: Brown,
Gold, Yellow
150g (5¼oz) sugarpaste: white

Equipment

Basic tools (see page 6)
Cotton thread: gold
Fan cutter: no. 495 (TT)
30-gauge floristry wire: gold
Miniature teardrop cutter or
template (see page 110)
Oval cutter set: 30mm-70mm (1⅛"
x 2¾")
Piping nozzle: no. 1
1mm-width ribbon: pale yellow
3mm-width ribbon: pale yellow
12.5cm (5") round cake card

Miniature Flowers and Foliage

5 twigs, various lengths
5 pointed tulips at various stages
(buds, half-open and open flowers)
5 rounded tulips at various stages
(buds, half-open and open flowers)
3 anemone flowers, 2 buds
3 monstera leaves
7 stems of eucalyptus leaves
3 iris flowers, 2 buds

Fan

1. Make up the pastillage following the instructions on the pack. Roll out on a non-stick board dusted with cornflour to a thickness of 1mm.

2. Cut out ten fan pieces using the cutter, then use a no. 1 piping nozzle to cut small holes at the top, bottom and where the ribbon will thread through the pieces. Cut out tiny teardrop shapes from the tips of the pieces using the cutter or template. Allow to dry overnight on a flat surface.

3. Bind the fan sections together using the gold wire and thread the yellow ribbon through the holes. Tie a piece of gold thread at both ends of the fan.

4. Paint the butterflies onto the fan with Yellow and Brown Edible Paint. Paint the edging on each section of the fan with Gold Edible Paint. Allow to dry.

Wedding Cake

5. Roll out some white sugarpaste to a thickness of 2cm. Cut out four ovals in different sizes, then cut out a section from each one using the same cutter to form a teardrop shape. Smooth over the cut edge with your finger and allow to dry.

Ornamental Fan Wedding Cake Actual Size

6. Cover the cake card with white sugarpaste and attach the 3mm pale yellow ribbon to the edge.

7. Place the 'cakes' onto the covered board and secure them in place with royal icing. Pipe a tiny snail's trail around the base of the cake using a no. 00 nozzle.

8. Attach 1mm pale yellow ribbon around the cakes using royal icing. Place the fan on top of the cake, again securing in place with royal icing.

9. Make the miniature flowers and arrange them in a loose 'L' shape in front of the cake. Paint a butterfly and a few dots on the board around the flowers.

TWIGS

Materials

SK Professional Metallic Lustre Dust
Food Colour: Antique Gold

Equipment

Basic tools (see page 6)
Floristry tape: white
33-gauge floristry wire: white

1. Cut a 33-gauge white floristry wire into six equal pieces. Tape down each piece of wire with $^1/_5$-width white floristry tape.

2. Tape the wires together and bend them to resemble twigs.

3. Dust the twigs with Antique Gold Metallic Dust Food Colour and pass over the steam from a kettle to set the colour.

TULIP

Materials

Basic materials (see page 6)
SK Professional Dust Food Colours:
Berberis, Holly/Ivy, Marigold, Rose,
Sunflower
SK Professional Paste Food Colour:
Leaf Green
SK Sugar Florist Paste (SFP): White

Equipment

Basic tools (see page 6)
Floristry tape: light green
30- and 33-gauge floristry wire: white
Mini oval cutter (smallest from set) (KB)
Miniature pointed tulip petal cutter or
template (see page 111)
Miniature tulip leaf cutters or
templates: set of 3 (see page 111)
Miniature stamens
Scientific wire: white

Pointed Petal Tulip: Pistil

1. Cut a 30-gauge white floristry wire into six equal pieces. Roll a tiny ball of White SFP, approximately 5mm across, moisten the tip of a length of wire with edible glue and insert it into the paste.

2. Form the paste into a sausage shape, then flatten the top of the pistil and cut it into three sections using a craft knife. Pinch the sections between your thumb and finger to give more definition.

Pointed Petal Tulip: Stamens

3. Trim the miniature stamens to 3mm. Roll a tiny ball of White SFP and insert a stamen into it. Form the paste into a flattened sausage shape and mark a line down the centre using a craft knife.

4. Repeat to make six stamens for each flower. Tape them around the pistil using $^1/_5$-width light green floristry tape.

5. Dust the flower centre with Sunflower Dust Food Colour.

Pointed Petals

6. Roll out some White SFP and cut out a petal shape using the cutter or template. Moisten the tip of a piece of scientific wire and insert it into the petal.

7. Mark two lines up the centre of the leaf using a cutting wheel. Mark veins from the centre outwards using the pointed end of a Dresden tool. Turn the petal over and mark a central vein using a cutting wheel.

8. Cup the petal using a miniature metal ball tool, then pinch the top between your finger and thumb.

9. Repeat this method to make six petals for each flower. Tape the petals around the flower centre with $^1/_5$-width light green floristry tape, arranging three in the first layer and three in-between them around the outside. To make a closed flower, tape the petals so that they are wrapped around the centre.

Rounded Petal Tulip: Flower Centre

10. Cut a 33-gauge wire into six equal pieces. Make a tiny hook in the end.

11. Roll a tiny ball of White SFP, approximately 5mm across. Moisten the wire hook and insert it into the paste. Mould the ball into an egg shape, then mark three sections in the paste using a cutting wheel.

12. Tape down the wire with $^1/_5$-width light green floristry tape.

13. Roll out some White SFP and cut out an oval using the smallest cutter in the set. Cut a tiny 'V' shape from the top using a craft knife.

14. Mark two lines up the centre of the petal using a cutting wheel then mark veins from the centre outwards using a Dresden tool. Turn the petal over and mark a central vein on the back. Cup the petal using a miniature metal ball tool.

15. Make another two petals in the same way for each flower. Moisten with edible glue and secure them to the flower centre.

Leaves

16. Colour some White SFP with Leaf Green Paste Food Colour. Roll out the paste and cut out a small, medium or large leaf shape (use a variety of sizes to give balance to the flowers). Mark veins on the leaf using a cutting wheel. Soften around the edge with a miniature metal ball tool.

17. Moisten the base of the leaf with edible glue and wrap it around the stem. Pinch and curl back the leaf with your fingers.

Both Tulips: Colouring

18. Dust the pointed petals from the edge inwards and from the centre outwards with Marigold and Berberis Dust Food Colours. Colour the rounded petals in the same way using Sunflower and Rose Dust Food Colours.

19. Dust the leaves with Holly/Ivy Paste Food Colour.

20. Pass the finished flowers through the steam from a kettle to set the colour.

ANEMONE

Materials

Basic materials (see page 6)
SK Professional Dust Food Colours:
Holly/Ivy, Jet Black, Lunar Blue
SK Professional Pollen Style Dust Food
Colour: Pale Yellow
SK Professional Paste Food Colours:
Blackberry, Leaf Green
SK Sugar Florist Paste (SFP): White

Equipment

Basic tools (see page 6)
5-petal blossom cutter: mini (CC)
5-petal blossom cutter: no. 100 (TT)
Craft dust: deep purple
Floristry tape: light green
33-gauge floristry wire: white
Miniature anemone leaf cutter or
template (see page 111)
Miniature stamens: white

Flower Centre

1. Cut a 33-gauge white floristry
    wire into six equal pieces. Colour
    a small amount of SFP with
    Blackberry Paste Food Colour
    and roll a small ball. Moisten the
    tip of a piece of wire with edible
    glue and insert the wire into the
    ball of paste.

2. Paint the miniature stamens
    with Blackberry Paste Food
    Colour and allow to dry. When
    dry, trim to 3mm.

3. Mix some Pale Yellow Pollen
    and Jet Black Dust Food Colours
    together in a palette. Pick up
    one stamen at a time using
    tweezers. Moisten the tip of the
    stamens with edible glue and
    dip them into the black pollen
    mixture. You will need to make
    ten stamens for each flower.

4. Tape the stamens around the
    black flower centre with $^1/_5$-
    width light green floristry tape.

Alternatively, trim the stamens
to 2mm and use craft glue
to secure them to the flower
centre.

Petals

5. Roll out some White SFP and
    cut out a mini blossom shape
    using the cutter. Use a craft knife
    to divide the petals further by
    cutting in towards the centre.

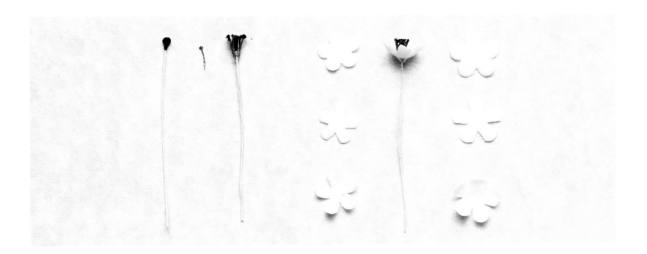

6. Using a miniature metal ball tool, soften the edges and give the petals a pointed shape by running the tool up the sides of each petal.

7. Moisten the centre of the blossom and thread it up the wire to meet the flower centre.

8. Make a second set of petals in the same way, this time using the slightly larger blossom cutter. Attach beneath and in-between the first layer of petals.

Bud

9. Prepare a flower centre without stamens. Add the first layer of petals using the same method as before.

10. Thread the petals up the wire and wrap one around the centre. Wrap the next but one petal around the centre and continue with alternate petals until all five are closed around the centre.

11. Tape down the stem with $^1/_5$-width floristry tape.

Leaves

12. Colour some White SFP a pale Holly/Ivy colour. Roll out the paste and cut out a poppy leaf shape using the cutter or template.

13. Soften around the edge of the leaf using a miniature metal ball tool then mark veins using a craft knife. Repeat to make four leaves for each flower.

14. Moisten the base of each leaf with edible glue and attach to the stem. The leaves on the buds should be further up the stem than those on the open flowers.

Colouring

15. Dust the anemone petals with deep purple craft dust from the edge inwards, leaving the central area white. Dust the very edges with Lunar Blue Dust Food Colour.

16. Dust the leaves with Holly/Ivy Dust Food Colour.

17. Pass the finished flowers through steam to set the colour.

MONSTERA

Materials

Basic materials (see page 6)
SK Professional Dust Food Colours:
Holly/Ivy, Sunflower
SK Professional Paste Food Colour:
Leaf Green
SK Sugar Florist Paste (SFP): White

Equipment

Basic tools (see page 6)
32-gauge floristry wire: green
Floristry tape: moss green
Miniature monstera leaf cutter or
template (see page 111)

1. Cut a 32-gauge green floristry wire into eight equal pieces.

2. Colour some White SFP pale green using a little Leaf Green Paste Food Colour. Roll out the paste on a non-stick board, leaving a ridge down the centre and cut out the leaf shape. Moisten a piece of wire with edible glue and insert it into the leaf.

3. Vein the leaf using a wheel tool then pinch it from the back to secure it to the wire. Place the leaf on a petal pad and soften around the edge using a miniature metal ball tool. Turn the leaf over and soften just inside the edge using the smallest end of the ball tool.

Colouring

4. Dust over the veins with Sunflower Dust Food Colour, then brush some Holly/Ivy Dust Food Colour from the edges inwards. Pass through the steam from a kettle and allow to dry.

5. Dip the leaf in ½-strength confectioners' glaze and allow to dry.

EUCALYPTUS 'BABY BLUE'

Materials

Basic materials (see page 6)
SK Professional Dust Food Colours:
Blackberry, Edelweiss, Holly/Ivy
SK Professional Paste Food Colour:
Sunflower
SK Sugar Florist Paste (SFP): White

Equipment

Basic tools (see page 6)
Craft dust: aubergine
Floristry tape: white
35-gauge floristry wire: white
Piping nozzle: no. 3

Leaves

1. Cut a 35-gauge white floristry wire into five equal pieces.

2. Colour some White SFP with a little Sunflower Paste Food Colour to make a pale yellow colour. Roll out the paste and cut out two tiny circles using the tip of a no. 3 piping nozzle.

3. Place the two circles on a non-stick board so that they overlap. Press the paste with your fingertip to join them together and thin the paste. Soften around the edge using a miniature metal ball tool.

4. Moisten the centre of the shape with edible glue. Thread it up a piece of wire to the top and pinch the base of the shape to secure it in place.

5. Repeat the same method, adding several leaves all the way down the stem.

Colouring

6. Mix together Holly/Ivy, Blackberry and Edelweiss Dust Food Colours and use this to dust the leaves. Dust the edges of the leaves and the stem with aubergine craft dust.

7. Pass the leaves through the steam from a kettle and allow to dry. Brush with ½-strength confectioners' glaze. (Alternatively, you can use an edible spray varnish if preferred.)

IRIS

Materials

Basic materials (see page 6)
SK Professional Dust Food Colours:
Holly/Ivy, Sunflower
SK Professional Paste Food Colour:
Leaf Green
SK Sugar Florist Paste (SFP): White

Equipment

Basic tools (see page 6)
Craft dusts: African violet, deep purple
Daisy cutter: no. 107 (TT)
33-gauge floristry wire: white
Floristry tape: light green
Iris cutters: set of 2 midi (KB)
Miniature iris calyx cutter or template (see page 111)
Miniature iris leaf cutter or template (see page 111)

Buds

1. Cut a 33-gauge white floristry wire into six equal pieces. Take one piece and make a tiny hook at the end.

2. Roll a ball of White SFP, approximately 3mm in diameter, and model it into a teardrop shape. Moisten the wire hook with edible glue and insert it into the pointed end of the teardrop. Model the paste with your fingers to create a narrow base and a point at the top.

3. Roll out some White SFP and cut out a tri-lobed shape using the iris cutter. Place the petal on a petal pad and soften around the edges using a miniature metal ball tool. Use the pointed end of a Dresden tool to frill the edges of the petals, pulling the tool towards the edges from the centre.

4. Brush the back of the petals with edible glue and insert the wired teardrop through the centre, glue-side up. Wrap the petals around the teardrop so that the textured side is showing.

5. Tape down the wire with ½-width light green floristry tape.

Open Flower

6. Cut a 33-gauge white floristry wire into six equal pieces and make a flower centre, as before.

7. Roll out some White SFP and cut

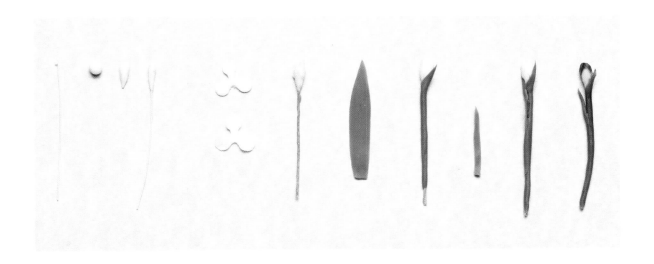

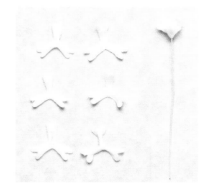

out the inner iris petal shape. Cut a 'V' shape from the tip of each of the three petals using a craft knife.

8. Soften around the edge of the petals using a miniature metal ball tool. Frill the top of the petals using the pointed end of a Dresden tool.

9. Turn the petals over and mark a central vein down each petal using the Dresden tool. Turn the petals back over and use a ball tool to mark two softened lines along the length of each petal. Pinch along the straight part of the petals using tweezers.

10. Moisten in the centre of the petals with edible glue, thread the shape up the wired centre and pinch the base to secure it in place. Curl in the top of the petals to form the flower shape.

11. Roll out some White SFP and cut out a daisy shape using the cutter. Cut the shape into individual petals (you will need three petals per flower) and soften each one with a ball tool. Pinch the rounded end of the petals between your thumb and finger.

12. Moisten the pointed end of each petal and secure them in-between the other three petals.

13. Roll out some White SFP and cut out the outer petal shape using the cutter. Soften the petals using a miniature ball tool.

14. Turn the petals over and mark a central vein on each one using the pointed end of a Dresden tool. Turn the back over again and mark two lines up the length of each petal using the ball tool. Turn the petals back over and frill the top part of the petals using the pointed end of a Dresden tool.

15. Moisten the centre of the petals with edible glue and thread the shape up the wire to meet the other petals.

Calyx

16. Colour some White SFP a pale shade of Holly/Ivy. Roll out the paste and cut out a calyx shape using the cutter or template.

17. Place the calyx on a petal pad and soften around the edges using a miniature metal ball tool.

18. Moisten the inside of the calyx with edible glue and wrap it around the flower or bud.

Leaves

19. Roll out some Holly/Ivy-coloured SFP and cut out the leaf shape using the miniature leaf cutter or template. Place the leaf on a petal pad and soften around the edges using a miniature metal ball tool.

20. Moisten the inside of the leaf with edible glue and attach to the stem. Pinch along the leaf to give it shape.

Colouring

21. Dust up the centre of each petal with Sunflower Dust Food Colour, then dust the remaining areas with African violet craft dust. Finally, add some deep purple craft dust on the edges.

22. Dust the calyx and leaves with Holly/Ivy Dust Food Colour. Pass the stems through the steam from a kettle to set the colour.

Assembly

1. Roll a 1cm diameter ball of white sugarpaste and secure this to the base tier of the cake using edible glue.

2. Use the irises and tulips to create the main shape of the bouquet. Starting with two buds, make an open 'L' shape by pushing the ends of the wires into the ball of sugarpaste. Add more irises and tulips to make a three-dimensional 'L' shape, keeping the open flowers towards the centre.

3. Arrange the anemones and stems of eucalyptus, keeping them within the 'L' shape. Add the monstera leaves at the base of the spray and finally arrange the twigs in the gaps between the flowers at the back of the arrangement.

Autumn Pixie

PIXIE ON APPLE

Materials

Basic materials (see page 6)
Demerara sugar
50g (1¾oz) SK Instant Mix Royal Icing
400g (14oz) SK Mexican Modelling
Paste (MMP): White
SK Professional Dust Food Colours:
Berberis, Bulrush, Jet Black, Lichen
Glow, Lilac, Marigold, Sunflower
SK Professional Liquid Food Colours:
Berberis, Bulrush, Sunflower, Vine
SK Professional Metallic Lustre Dust
Food Colour: Antique Gold
SK Professional Paste Food Colours:
Berberis, Bulrush, Chestnut, Rose,
Sunflower, Vine
10g (¼oz) SK Sugar Florist Paste (SFP):
White

Equipment

Basic tools (see page 6)
Butterfly veiner
6mm (¼") circle cutter
Fairy head mould (HP)
Floristry tape: brown
26-gauge floristry wire: white
Piping nozzle: no. 1
5cm (2") styrofoam ball (CEL)
Templates: tunic, wing (see page 111)
Wooden skewer

Miniature Flowers and Foliage

8 toadstools: 3 red, 5 white
4 spider chrysanthemums, 6 half-
open flowers, 3 buds
7 spray mum chrysanthemums, 4
half-open flowers, 2 buds
16 chrysanthemum leaves
15 oak leaves
8 acorns

Apple

1. Using a rolling pin, mould the styrofoam ball to form an apple shape. Narrow the sides towards the bottom, then push a small rolling pin into the top to make an indent.

2. Colour some White MMP with a little Sunflower Paste Food Colour to make a pale yellow tone. Roll out the paste to a thickness of 5mm and brush the top surface with edible glue.

3. Carefully lift up the paste and wrap it around the apple shape. Smooth over the shape with your hands, gathering the excess paste at the bottom. Cut off the excess folds of paste with a pair of scissors, then smooth the surface with your hands using warm, boiled water.

4. Cut a 3cm length of 26-gauge floristry wire and bend the top to one side and then back on itself to form a 'T' shape. Tape over the wire with brown floristry tape, glue the end and insert it into the top of the apple to form the stalk.

5. Push a wooden skewer into the base of the apple, then push the other end into a polystyrene block or similar so that the apple is suspended. Allow to dry.

6. When the apple is dry, paint it with a mixture of Vine and Sunflower Liquid Food Colours diluted with clear alcohol. Allow to dry.

Autumn Pixie Actual Size

7. Dilute some Rose and Bulrush Paste Food Colours with clear alcohol to make a colour wash and paint over the apple to give a reddish-brown colour.

Pixie's Head

8. Add a hint of Berberis Paste Food Colour to a ball of White MMP to make a pale flesh colour.

9. Roll a 1cm diameter ball of the coloured MMP and push into the fairy head mould. Remove from the mould and push a cocktail stick into the neck.

10. Open up the mouth using a craft knife then define the nostrils with a cocktail stick.

11. Roll two tiny balls of the flesh-coloured paste and form them into pointed ears. Secure them to the sides of the head using edible glue.

12. Paint inside the eyes with diluted Berberis Liquid Food Colour. Using a very fine paintbrush, paint around the eyes and eyelids with Bulrush Liquid Food Colour, then add the eyebrows and pupils.

13. Paint the mouth with Berberis Liquid Food Colour, then dust the cheeks and forehead with Berberis Dust Food Colour.

Hands

14. Roll a tiny sausage of the flesh-coloured MMP. Cut it in half and press the end of each piece flat to form the hand shapes.

15. Make a cut for each of the fingers and cut out a 'V' shape to make the thumb. Press into the palm using a miniature ball tool.

Legs

16. Add some Berberis and Chestnut Paste Food Colours to some White MMP.

17. Roll a sausage shape and cut it in half on the diagonal. Roll each piece between your thumb and finger to thin the ankle and knee areas, keeping the diagonal cut at the top. Shape the feet and bend at the knees into the required position.

Body

18. Colour some White MMP with Leaf Green and Bulrush Paste Food Colours to make the colour required for the clothing. Set aside half the paste to make the tunic later and reserve a small piece for the arms.

19. Roll the remaining paste into a small ball, then reshape this into a rectangle for the body. Indent the paste at the waist, then hollow out the neck and shoulder joints using a ball tool.

Arms

20. Roll a sausage shape of the coloured paste, cut the ends straight and make a diagonal cut in the centre for the arms. Make tiny holes in the straight end of each piece with a cocktail stick as this will make the surface easier to glue to the shoulders.

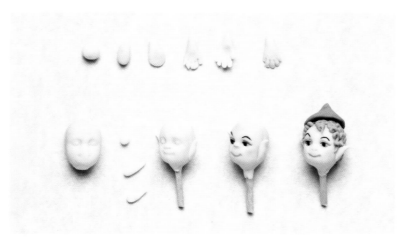

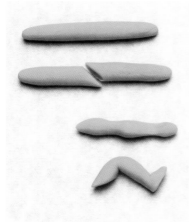

Clothing

21. To make the tunic, roll out the reserved Leaf Green/Bulrush-coloured paste and cut out the shape using the template. Remove a circle from the centre using a 6mm cutter then make a straight cut down from this using a cutting wheel. Mark stitches down the edges of the tunic using a Dresden tool. Keep the trimmings to make the hat later.

22. Mix some MMP with edible glue to form a thick paste and use this to attach the body to the apple. When it is held firmly in place, glue the legs to the body. Glue the tunic in place with the hole at the neck and the cut down the front. Mark two holes either side of the cut using a cocktail stick.

23. Brush some of the paste glue into the arm sockets and secure the arms in place. Do the same with the hands and hold in place until secure.

24. Trim the cocktail stick in the pixie's neck so that it protrudes by 1cm. Brush the cocktail stick and base of the head with the paste glue and insert it into the body.

25. Colour a small amount of royal icing with Bulrush and Berberis Liquid Food Colours and place it in a piping bag with a no. 1 piping nozzle. Pipe the hair onto the pixie and add two ties at the front of the tunic.

26. To make the acorn hat, mould a small piece of the Leaf Green/Bulrush-coloured paste into a circle with a point on the top. Secure it on top of the head.

Wings

27. Roll out the remaining pale flesh-coloured SFP thinly on a non-stick board greased with white vegetable fat. Cut out two wings using the template and a cutting wheel, vein in the butterfly veiner and allow to dry flat.

28. Dust the edges of the wings with Antique Gold Metallic Lustre Dust, then secure to the back of the pixie with the paste glue.

Tree Stump

29. Colour some MMP with Bulrush Paste Food Colour and mould into the shape of the stump.

30. Using a Dresden tool mark the top and sides of the tree stump to resemble wood, then dust with Jet Black, Lilac, Bulrush, Lichen Glow and Marigold Dust Food Colours.

31. When dry, brush ½-strength confectioners' glaze around the sizes of the tree stump.

32. Secure the apple and pixie to the tree stump with the paste glue. Sprinkle Demerara sugar around the base of the tree stump, then arrange the flowers and toadstools around the apple.

TOADSTOOL

Materials

Basic materials (see page 6)
SK Professional Paste Food Colour:
Rose
SK Professional Dust Food Colours:
Bulrush, Marigold, Rose
SK Sugar Florist Paste (SFP): White

Equipment

Basic tools (see page 6)
30-gauge floristry wire: white

Red Toadstool

1. Roll a tiny piece of White SFP into a sausage shape and cut it in half. Take one half and pinch the end to create a wide, fanned end then place it on a non-stick board and mark around the edge using a Dresden tool.

2. Cut a 30-gauge white floristry wire into eight equal pieces. Take a piece of wire, moisten the end with edible glue and insert it into the opposite end to the fanned paste.

3. Join the two pieces of paste back together with the fanned part in the centre to form the stalk. The wire should protrude from one end. Mark a few vertical lines down the length of the paste using a craft knife and bend the stalk to form a slight curve. Allow to dry.

4. Roll a tiny piece of White SFP into a ball, then flatten it and pinch around the edge to make a cap shape.

5. Using a craft knife, mark lines from the centre of the paste to the edge. Cut a few small 'V' shapes from the edge of the paste.

6. Press in the centre of the paste on the same side with a flexible CelStick, then turn it over and secure it to the stalk with edible glue.

7. Colour some SFP with Rose Paste Food Colour. Roll a small piece of this paste into a ball and secure it to the top of the toadstool with edible glue. Using your finger and thumb, work the paste down to cover the cap shape.

8. Dust the top of the toadstool with Rose Dust Food Colour, then colour the underside of the cap and the stalk with Bulrush Dust Food Colour.

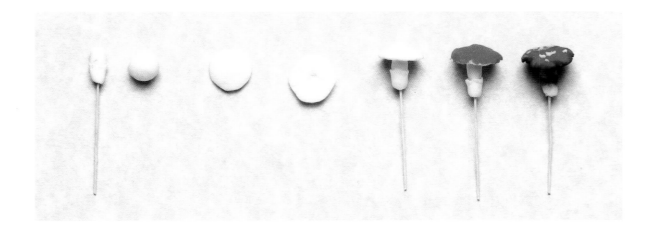

9. Thinly roll out some White SFP and break off tiny pieces using a Dresden tool. Attach these to the top of the toadstool with edible glue.

10. Pass the completed toadstool through the steam from a kettle to set the colour. Allow to dry, then cut off the protruding wire from the base of the stalk.

White Toadstool

11. To make a small, white toadstool, roll a small sausage of White SFP for the stalk and insert a moistened piece of 30-gauge wire into the end. Mark lines down the paste using a craft knife and curve it slightly.

12. Make a cap in the same way as for the red toadstool but make it more slim and pointed than before. Moisten the centre with edible glue and attach the stalk.

13. Dust the top of the cap with Marigold Dust Food Colour, then add a little Bulrush on the edge of the cap and in the middle of the stem.

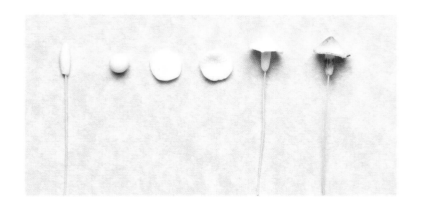

SPIDER CHRYSANTHEMUM

Materials

Basic materials (see page 6)
SK Professional Dust Food Colours:
Daffodil, Holly/Ivy
SK Professional Paste Food Colours:
Daffodil, Leaf Green
SK Sugar Florist Paste (SFP): White

Equipment

Basic tools (see page 6)
5-point calyx cutter: micro (CEL)
Chrysanthemum leaf cutter (CCC)
Daisy cutters: micro and mini (CEL)
Daisy cutter: no. 107 (TT)
Floristry tape: moss green
32-gauge floristry wires: green
30-gauge floristry wires: white
Glass-headed pin
Leaf veiner: micro (CP)

Flower Centre

1. Cut a 30-gauge white floristry wire into eight equal pieces. Using tweezers, make a loop at one end of a piece of wire to make a ski stick shape. Brush this with edible glue.

2. Colour some White SFP with Daffodil Paste Food Colour. Roll a tiny ball and press it onto the wire loop. Mark lines around the paste from the centre using a craft knife and push into the centre using a flexible CelStick. Dust with Daffodil Dust Food Colour.

Petals

3. Roll out the yellow-coloured SFP and cut out a daisy shape using the micro cutter. Snip each petal in half using fine, pointed scissors.

4. Place the petals on a petal pad and soften with a miniature metal ball tool. Pull the tool from the centre of the petals to the tip to curl them in and give the flower a cupped shape.

5. Moisten the centre of the petals with edible glue, then thread the

wired flower centre down through the petals. Wrap the petals around the centre to make a bud.

6. To make an open flower, repeat steps 1 to 5. Cut a miniature daisy shape and cup the petals with a ball tool. Thread this up the wire and secure to the flower with edible glue. Repeat to make a third layer using the largest cutter (no. 107).

Calyx

7. Colour some White SFP with Leaf Green Paste Food Colour. Roll out the paste and cut out a calyx shape using the micro cutter.

8. Place the calyx on a petal pad and soften around the edge with a miniature metal ball tool. Moisten the centre with edible glue, thread it up the wire and secure it to the flower or bud.

9. Make another calyx in the same way and secure it to the first one so that the sepals are in-between those of the first layer.

Bud

10. Make a flower centre in the same way as before from White SFP. Mark lines down the sides and push into the centre, as before.

Colouring

11. Dust the petals with Daffodil Dust Food Colour. Dust the calyx and buds with Holly/Ivy Dust Food Colour. Pass the flowers through the steam from a kettle to set the colour.

Leaves

12. Roll out some Leaf Green-coloured SFP, leaving a ridge down the centre. Cut out a leaf shape using the chrysanthemum leaf cutter.

13. Cut a 32-gauge green floristry wire into eight equal pieces. Moisten a piece of wire with edible glue and insert it into the central ridge of the leaf.

14. Vein the leaf using the veiner, then place it on a petal and soften with a miniature metal ball tool. Pinch the bottom of the leaf from the back to secure it firmly on the wire.

15. Dust the leaf with Holly/Ivy Dust Food Colour, then dust the edges with Daffodil. Pass through the steam from a kettle.

16. Dip the leaf into ½-strength confectioners' glaze and allow to dry.

17. Tape the stem with ⅓-width moss green floristry tape.

SPRAY MUM CHRYSANTHEMUM

Materials

Basic materials (see page 6)
SK Professional Dust Food Colours:
Bulrush, Cyclamen, Holly/Ivy,
Sunflower
SK Professional Paste Food Colours:
Berberis, Holly/Ivy, Sunflower
SK Sugar Florist Paste (SFP): White

Equipment

Basic tools (see page 6)
5-point calyx cutter: micro (CEL)
Floristry tape: moss green
32-gauge floristry wires: green
Miniature chrysanthemum leaf cutter
or template (see page 111)
Rounded 6-petal flower cutter (CCC)

Flower Centre

1. Cut a 32-gauge white floristry wire into eight equal pieces. Take one piece and make a loop in one end to resemble a ski stick.

2. Colour some White SFP with Sunflower Paste Food Colour. Roll a tiny ball and secure it to the wire loop with edible glue. Make lots of tiny holes in the paste using a scriber and push down into the centre using a flexible CelStick.

3. Dust the flower centre with Sunflower Dust Food Colour.

Petals

4. Colour some White SFP with Berberis Paste Food Colour. Roll out the paste on a non-stick board and cut out the rounded daisy shape using the cutter.

5. Place the petals on a petal pad and, using the pointed end of a Dresden tool, push into each petal and pull out to the end to make a pointed tip.

6. Moisten the centre of the petals with edible glue and thread the petals up the wire to meet the flower centre.

7. Repeat the same method to make another set of petals and attach them beneath and in-between the first layer.

8. Dust the top of the flower with a mixture of Cyclamen and Bulrush Dust Food Colours.

Bud

9. Make a flower centre in the same way as for the flower. Roll out some Berberis-coloured SFP and cut out the rounded daisy shape. Cut each of the petals in two using fine, pointed scissors.

10. Place the petals on a petal pad and soften them using a Dresden tool. Moisten the centre with edible glue and thread them up the wire. Wrap the petals around the flower centre.

11. Dust the bud with a mixture of Cyclamen and Bulrush Dust Food Colours.

Calyx

12. Roll out some Holly/Ivy-coloured SFP and cut out two calyx shapes using the micro calyx cutter. Place them on a petal pad and soften the edges using a miniature metal ball tool.

13. Moisten the centre of each calyx with edible glue and attach them to the base of the flower or bud so that the sepals are positioned in-between each other. Dust the calyx with Holly/Ivy Dust Food Colour.

14. Pass the finished flower or bud through the steam from a kettle to set the colour. Tape down the stem with ¼-width floristry tape.

Leaves

15. Make the leaves in the same way as for the spider chrysanthemum.

OAK LEAVES AND ACORNS

Materials

Basic materials (see page 6)
SK Professional Paste Food Colours:
Bulrush, Marigold
SK Professional Dust Food Colours:
Berberis, Bulrush, Leaf Green, Marigold
SK Sugar Florist Paste (SFP): White

Equipment

Basic tools (see page 6)
30- and 35-gauge floristry wires: white
Floristry tape: brown
Leaf veiner: micro (CP)
Lighter or matches
Miniature oak leaf cutters or templates (see page 111)

Oak Leaves

1. Cut a piece of 35-gauge white floristry wire into eight equal pieces.

2. Colour some White SFP with Marigold and Bulrush Paste Food Colours to make a golden brown colour. Roll out the paste, leaving a ridge down the centre, and cut out the leaf shape using the cutter or template.

3. Moisten a piece of wire with edible glue and insert it into the ridge of the leaf. Vein in the leaf veiner, then pinch the base of the leaf to secure it to the wire.

4. Place the leaf on a petal pad and soften around the edge using a miniature metal ball tool.

5. Dust the leaf with Marigold, Berberis, Leaf Green and Bulrush Dust Food Colours. Use more Leaf Green on the younger leaves and more Bulrush on the mature leaves.

6. Pass the leaf through the steam from a kettle to set the colour and allow to dry.

7. Dip the leaf into ½-strength confectioners' glaze and allow to dry.

8. To add a finishing touch, heat a 30-gauge floristry wire in the flame of a lighter or match and mark the leaf so that it looks as if insects have been eating it.

Acorns

9. Paint the top part of a piece of 35-gauge wire with Bulrush Paste Food Colour.

10. Roll a tiny piece of the golden brown-coloured SFP made earlier into an egg shape. Moisten the end of the Bulrush-

coloured wire with edible glue and insert the wire into the paste so that the brown tip protrudes from the top.

11. Roll a tiny ball of the golden brown-coloured SFP and push into the middle with a miniature metal ball tool to make a cup shape. Moisten inside the cup with edible glue and thread the wire down through the middle so that the acorn sits in the cup. Mark tiny holes in the cup using a scriber.

12. Dust the acorn with Berberis, Leaf Green and Bulrush Dust Food Colours. Use more Leaf Green on the young acorns and more Bulrush on the older ones.

13. Pass the acorn over the steam from a kettle and allow to dry before dipping into ½-strength confectioners' glaze.

Buds

14. Tape a piece of wire with ¼-width brown floristry tape, forming the tape into a bud shape at the top.

Assembly

1. Tape the chrysanthemums and buds to create stems of varying lengths. Tape the stems together to form a triangular shape, positioning the open flowers in the centre and the buds towards the edges. Position the arrangement to one side of the apple. Place one spray mum chrysanthemum in the hand of the pixie.

2. Make three twigs of oak leaves and acorns, varying in length, and tape them together to make a branch. Keep a couple of leaves and acorns loose. Place the twigs on the other side of the apple and scatter the loose leaves and acorn around the base.

3. Secure the toadstools to the tree stump in the spaces between the flowers and leaves, singly and in pairs.

Exotic Wedding Cake

TWO-TIER WEDDING CAKE

Materials

20g (¾oz) apricot glaze
Basic materials (see page 6)
50g (1¾oz) SK Instant Mix Professional
Royal Icing
100g (3½oz) SK Marzipan
SK Professional Paste Food Colour:
Chestnut
15cm (6") SK Square Rich Fruit Cake
(or smaller if possible)
150g (5¼oz) sugarpaste: white

Equipment

Angle-poise lamp
Basic tools (see page 6)
18cm (7") round cake card
Gold beads
Miniature tube pillar
4cm and 8.5cm oval cutters
Piping nozzle: no. 00
1mm- and 3mm-width ribbon:
golden brown
Templates: lace pieces, ovals (see
page 110)
Tracing paper
Wax paper

Miniature Flowers and Foliage

7 cymbidium orchids
7 hosta leaves
8 stems of ruscus leaves, various
lengths
7 clusters of viburnum berries, various
sizes (see Decorative Wedding Cake
Plaque project, page 25)

Cake Board

1. Using the templates as a guide, cut the round cake card into two oval shapes, one large and one small.

2. Colour some white sugarpaste with a little Chestnut Paste Food Colour to make a pale ivory tone. Brush the larger oval cake board with clear alcohol, roll out the sugarpaste to a thickness of 2mm and cover the board. Smooth the surface and trim neatly around the edge.

3. Secure a length of 3mm-width ribbon around the edge of the board using a little royal icing or sugarpaste mixed to a paste with a little cooled, boiled water.

Cake

4. Slice the cake in half horizontally to create two shallow squares (each piece should be approximately 2cm deep). Using the oval cutters, cut out the top and bottom tiers of the cake.

5. Brush the two miniature oval cakes with apricot glaze. Roll out some marzipan on a non-stick board dusted with icing sugar to a thickness of 5mm. Cover both cakes and leave to dry overnight.

Exotic Wedding Cake Actual Size

6. Place the small cake on the small cake card. Moisten the surface of both marzipanned cakes with clear alcohol, roll out the sugarpaste to a thickness of 5mm and cover the cakes. Smooth over the top and sides and trim neatly around the base. Place the larger cake on the covered cake card.

7. Attach golden brown ribbon around the base of each cake using a little paste glue or royal icing.

Lacework

8. Trace the five lace pieces onto a piece of tracing paper. Secure the patterns to a spare cake card, then attach a piece of wax paper over the top with masking tape.

9. Make up the professional royal icing following the instructions on the pack and fill a piping bag fitted with a no. 00 piping nozzle. Pipe the lace designs onto the wax paper, then place under an angle-poise lamp to dry.

10. When the icing is completely dry, dust the top part of each lace piece with Cyclamen Dust Food Colour. Once all the pieces are dusted, carefully release the pieces from the wax paper.

11. Pipe a thin line of royal icing along the edge of each lace piece and attach them to the sides of the cakes.

12. Fill the miniature pillar with gold beads and assemble the tiers. Arrange the flowers on the cakes.

CYMBIDIUM ORCHID

Materials

Basic materials (see page 6)
SK Professional Dust Food Colours:
Cyclamen, Lilac, Sunflower
SK Professional Liquid Food Colour:
Cyclamen
SK Professional Paste Food Colour:
Sunflower
SK Sugar Florist Paste (SFP): White

Equipment

Basic tools (see page 6)
Floristry tape: Nile green
35-gauge floristry wire: white
Miniature cymbidium orchid cutters
or templates (see page 111)
Paintbrush: no. 00000

Column

1. Cut a 35-gauge white floristry wire into eight equal pieces. Make a hook in the end of one of the wire pieces. Roll a tiny ball of White SFP, moisten the tip of a length of wire with edible glue and insert it into the paste.

2. Mould the ball of paste into a teardrop shape, then press into one side of the paste and pinch the back with your fingers to form the column shape. Gently bend the top over as you work to form a curve.

3. Colour some White SFP with Sunflower Paste Food Colour. Roll a tiny ball of the yellow paste, approximately 0.5mm across, and attach it to the tip of the column using edible glue. Divide the ball in two using a craft knife.

4. Dilute a little Cyclamen Liquid Food Colour with clear alcohol. Using a no. 00000 paintbrush, paint tiny dots onto the inside of the column.

5. Dust the top of the column with Sunflower Dust Food Colour and the back with Cyclamen.

Throat

6. Roll out some White SFP and cut out the shape for the throat using the cutter or template. Place the shape on a petal pad and soften around the edges using a miniature metal ball tool.

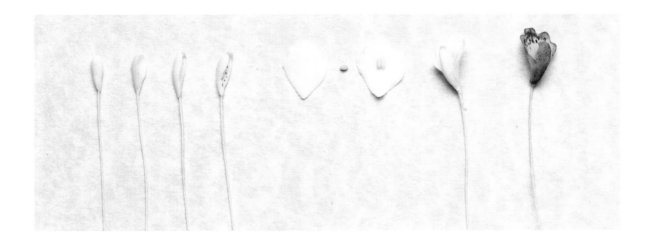

7. Roll two tiny sausages of yellow paste and attach these vertically down the centre of the throat using edible glue.

8. Brush a little edible glue along the two straight sides of the throat and wrap it around the column. Curl back the top to form a natural shape.

9. Using the diluted Cyclamen colour and the no. 00000 paintbrush, paint the scalloped area inside the throat.

10. Dust the two strips of yellow paste inside the throat with Sunflower Dust Food Colour, then dust the back of the throat with a mixture of Cyclamen and Lilac Dust Food Colours.

Petals

11. Roll out some White SFP, leaving a ridge down the centre. Using the cutters or templates, cut out the petals one at a time, starting with two wing petals, followed by the top petal and two leg petals.

12. Moisten the end of a piece of 35-gauge white floristry wire and insert it into the ridge. Place the petal on a petal pad and soften around the edges from the base to the tip using a miniature metal ball tool. Pinch the bottom and top of the petal between your finger and thumb.

13. Dust each petal with a mixture of Cyclamen and Lilac Dust Food Colours. Using a no. 00000 paintbrush and diluted Cyclamen Liquid Food Colour, paint lines from the base of the petal to the tip and allow to dry.

14. Tape the petals to the throat, starting with the wings, followed by the top petal between them, then finally add the leg petals either side of the throat.

15. Tape down the stem with ¼-width Nile green floristry tape. Pass the completed flower through the steam from a kettle to set the colour.

Buds

16. Roll a tiny ball of White SFP into a teardrop shape. Make a tiny hook in the end of a 35-gauge white floristry wire, moisten with edible glue and insert it into the rounded end of the teardrop.

17. Mark three lines down the sides of the teardrop, then pinch each section between your thumb and finger.

18. Tape down the wire with $^1/_5$-width Nile green floristry tape. Bend the top of the wire over so that the bud is pointing downwards.

19. Dust the bud with a mixture of Cyclamen and Lilac Dust Food Colours and pass through the steam from a kettle to set the colour.

HOSTA

Materials

Basic materials (see page 6)
SK Professional Paste Food Colours:
Holly/Ivy, Leaf Green
SK Sugar Florist Paste (SFP): White

Equipment

Basic tools (see page 6)
Floristry tape: moss green
32-gauge floristry wire: green
Miniature hosta leaf cutters or templates (see page 111)

1. Cut a 32-gauge green floristry wire into eight equal pieces.

2. Colour some White SFP with Holly/Ivy Paste Food Colour and make a teardrop shape. Make another teardrop from White SFP and press the two together so that the green teardrop is just below and in front of the white one.

3. Roll out the paste so that the green is on top with a white edge surrounding it, leaving a ridge down the centre. Cut out the hosta leaf shape using either the large or small cutter or template. Make sure the leaf is green with a white edge.

4. Insert a moistened length of 32-gauge floristry wire into the ridge. Place the leaf on a petal pad and soften the edges using a miniature metal ball tool. Mark veins down the front of the leaf using a plain cutting wheel.

5. Dilute some Leaf Green Paste Food Colour with clear alcohol and paint both sides of the leaf. Allow to dry, then over-paint both sides with diluted Holly/Ivy Paste Food Colour. Allow to dry.

6. Dip the finished leaf into ½-strength confectioners' glaze and allow to dry. Tape down the stem with $^1/_5$-width moss green floristry tape.

RUSCUS

Materials

Basic materials (see page 6)
SK Professional Dust Food Colour:
Forest Green
SK Professional Paste Food Colour:
Leaf Green
SK Sugar Florist Paste (SFP): White

Equipment

Basic tools (see page 6)
Floristry tape: dark green
Miniature ruscus leaf cutter or
template (see page 111)
Scientific wire: white

1. Colour some White SFP with Leaf Green Paste Food Colour. Roll out the paste on a non-stick board, leaving a ridge down the centre, and cut out a leaf shape.

2. Cut a 5cm length of scientific wire. Moisten the end with edible glue and insert it into the ridge.

3. Place the leaf on a petal pad and soften around the edges with a miniature metal ball tool. Mark veins from the base of the leaf to the tip using a plain cutting wheel. Pinch the leaf at the top to give a sharper point.

4. Make five or seven leaves per stem and glue the wires together with high-tack craft glue. Tape over the wire with ¹/₆-width dark green floristry tape.

VIBURNUM BERRY

For instructions on making the viburnum berries, see page 25.

Assembly

1. For the front-facing arrangement on the top tier, roll a tiny ball of the ivory-coloured sugarpaste to hold the wires. Insert three ruscus stems into the paste, one at the top and one on either side to make a triangular shape. Add three cymbidium orchids in the centre, then fill in any gaps with three stems of viburnum berries and three cymbidium orchid buds. Finally, insert three hosta leaves into the back of the arrangement, one at the top and one on either side.

2. To make the oval arrangement on the lower tier, roll a small ball of sugarpaste for the wires. Insert two short ruscus stems into the front and back of the paste and two longer stems into the sides to make a flat oval. Add another stem in the top. Add three cymbidium orchid bud stems, one on each side and one in the centre. Add four orchids around the front, central area and fill in the gaps with four stems of viburnum berries. Finally, insert four hosta leaves into the back of the arrangement.

A Trio of Roses Wedding Cake

WEDDING CAKE IN BIRD CAGE

Materials

Basic materials (see page 6)
SK Professional Paste Food Colour:
Daffodil
100g (3½oz) sugarpaste: white

Equipment

Basic tools (see page 6)
Craft glitter: orange
Floristry tape: white
Ornamental bird cage (or similar to
display cake)
Piece of light fabric, e.g. organdy
Ribbon: white chiffon
1mm (¹⁄₂₅") width ribbon: yellow
1cm, 2cm, 3cm and 4cm (³⁄₈", ¾", 1¹⁄₈"
and 1½") round cake dummies
5cm (2") round cake card

Miniature Flowers and Foliage

20 old-fashioned roses, various sizes
40-45 rose leaves
10-12 rambling roses, 10-12 buds, 20-
25 leaves
10-12 wild roses, 10-12 buds
12-15 jasmine flowers, 20-25 buds,
70-75 leaves
10-12 stems of freesias, various sizes

1. Colour the sugarpaste with
    Daffodil Paste Food Colour to
    make a pale yellow tone. Brush
    the cake dummies and cake card
    with edible glue and cover with
    the yellow sugarpaste. Stack the
    cakes on the card, securing them
    in place with edible glue.

2. Make an 'S' shape flower spray to
    decorate the top of the cake and
    place individual flowers on the
    lower tiers. Attach a butterfly to
    the edge of the third tier using
    edible glue.

3. Place the cake into the bird cage
    and arrange a piece of organdy
    fabric around it. Decorate the
    cage with sprays of flowers,
    butterflies and ribbon.

Miniature Wedding Cake Actual Size

A Trio of Roses Wedding Cake Actual Size

BUTTERFLIES

Materials

Basic materials (see page 6)

SK Professional Dust Food Colours: Berberis, Bluebell, Vine, Violet

SK Professional Metallic Lustre Dust Food Colours: Antique Gold, Burnt Copper, Silver, Snowflake

SK Sugar Florist Paste (SFP): White

Equipment

Basic tools (see page 6)

Butterfly cutter: micro (CP)

Craft glitter: orange

Miniature stamens

30-gauge paper-covered floristry wire: silver

Silk veining tool (HP)

1. Roll out some White SFP thinly and cut out a butterfly using the micro cutter. Texture and thin the wings using a silk veining tool.

2. Cut two miniature stamens to 3mm in length. Roll a 2mm diameter ball of White SFP into a long teardrop shape for the body, then mark the head using a Dresden tool. Moisten the cut ends of the stamens and insert them into the head for the feelers.

3. Moisten the back of the body with edible glue and secure the wings into position.

4. Cut a 30-gauge silver-covered wire into four equal pieces. Take one of the pieces, moisten the end with edible glue and push it into the underside of the butterfly's body. Allow to dry.

5. Make five butterflies altogether and dust them with the following colours: Burnt Copper Metallic Dust; Silver Metallic and Violet Dusts; Silver Metallic and Bluebell Dusts; Antique Gold Metallic and Berberis Dusts; and Snowflake Metallic and Vine Dusts. Leave one of the butterflies unwired for the cake decoration.

6. Moisten the edges of the wings with edible glue and dip them into orange glitter.

OLD-FASHIONED ROSE

Materials

Basic materials (see page 6)
SK Professional Dust Food Colours:
Edelweiss, Holly/Ivy, Sunflower
SK Professional Paste Food Colour:
Leaf Green
SK Sugar Florist Paste (SFP): White

Equipment

Basic tools (see page 6)
5-petal blossom cutters: nos. 98 and 100 (TT)
Calyx cutter: micro (FC)
Craft dust: apricot
Daisy cutter: mini (CEL)
Leaf veiner: micro (CP)

Floristry tape: light green
32-gauge floristry wire: green
30-gauge floristry wire: white
Miniature rose leaf cutters or templates: large, medium and small (see page 111)
Miniature stamens: white

Flower Centre

1. Cut a 30-gauge wire into eight equal pieces. Cut five miniature stamens in half and tape them to the wire using $^1/_5$-width white floristry tape. Trim off the excess length from the stamens as you tape down the wire.

2. Mix some Sunflower Dust Food Colour with clear alcohol and paint the stamens yellow. Allow to dry.

Petals

3. Roll out some White SFP and cut out a miniature daisy shape using the cutter. Make 1mm-2mm cuts in-between the petals using fine scissors.

3. Place the daisy shape on a petal pad and soften around the edges using a miniature metal ball tool. Working from the edges towards the centre, use the same tool to cup the blossom shape.

4. Make two more blossoms in the same way, thread the three layers of petals up the wire and secure them to the flower centre using edible glue. Make sure the petals of each layer can be seen in-between the other petals.

5. For a fully-open flower, roll out some White SFP and cut out two sets of inner petals using the no. 98 cutter and two sets of outer (slightly larger) petals using the no. 100 cutter. To make a half-open flower, simply cut out two of the larger blossoms (no. 100). Make 1mm cuts in-between each of the petals using fine, pointed scissors.

6. Place the petals on a petal pad and soften around the edges using a miniature metal ball tool. Use the ball tool in a circular motion on each petal to soften and cup the paste.

7. Brush a little edible glue in the centre of the blossom and thread it up the wire to the base of the flower. Repeat with the subsequent layers of petals, then gently curl back the edges of the outer petals.

Calyx

8. Colour some White SFP with Leaf Green Paste Food Colour. Roll a teardrop shape, then pinch out the paste around the base to make a Mexican hat shape.

9. Cut out the calyx with the bump of paste in the middle. Make tiny cuts in each sepal using a craft knife.

10. Place the calyx on a petal pad and soften around the edges with a miniature metal ball tool. Use the same tool to cup the calyx, then moisten the centre with edible glue and secure it to the base of the flower.

Colouring

11. Dust the centre of the flower with Sunflower Dust Food Colour, then dust the petals with apricot craft dust. Dust the calyx with Holly/Ivy Dust Food Colour and add a little of the apricot dust around the edge. Finally, dust the inside of the calyx with Edelweiss Dust Food Colour.

12. Pass the flower through the steam from a kettle to set the colour. Finish by taping the stem with ¼-width light green floristry tape.

Leaves

13. Cut a 32-gauge green floristry wire into eight equal pieces.

14. Roll out some Leaf Green-coloured SFP, leaving a ridge down the centre. Cut out the leaf shape using either the small, medium or large cutter or template and insert a wire moistened with edible glue into the ridge.

15. Vein the leaf in the veiner, then place it on a petal pad and soften around the edges using a miniature metal ball tool. Pinch the base of the leaf with your fingers to secure it to the wire.

16. Dust the edges of the leaves the same colours as the flower, then dust the front and back with Holly/Ivy Dust Food Colour.

17. Pass the leaf through the steam from a kettle to set the colour, then dip into ½-strength confectioners' glaze and allow to dry.

18. Make several leaves in various sizes, according to the size of spray you wish to create.

19. Tape the leaves in groups of either three or five using ⅕-width light green floristry tape. Position the largest leaf at the top (either large or medium) and one or two pairs of smaller leaves (medium or small) further down the stem.

RAMBLING ROSE

Materials

Basic materials (see page 6)
SK Professional Dust Food Colours:
Cyclamen, Edelweiss, Holly/Ivy, Pastel
Pink, Sunflower
SK Professional Paste Food Colour:
Leaf Green
SK Sugar Florist Paste (SFP): White

Equipment

Basic tools (see page 6)
5-blossom cutter: no. 100 (TT)
5-petal blossom cutters: mini and
micro (CEL)
Calyx cutter: mini (CEL)
Flat dusting brush
Floristry tape: light green

32-gauge floristry wire: green
30-gauge floristry wire: white
Miniature rose leaf cutters or
templates: large, medium and
small (see page 111)
Miniature stamens: white

Flower Centre

1. Cut a 30-gauge white floristry
   wire into eight equal pieces. Cut
   four miniature stamens in half,
   then tape them to the top of
   the wire using $^1/_5$-width white
   floristry tape. Trim away the
   excess length from the stamens
   as you tape down the wire.

Petals

2. Roll out some White SFP and cut
   out a 5-petal blossom using the
   micro cutter. Cut in-between

each of the petals using fine,
pointed scissors.

3. Place the blossom on a petal
   pad and soften around the
   edge using a miniature metal
   ball tool. Using the same tool,
   press into the paste from the
   sides of the petals to the tip to
   form a pointed shape.

4. Moisten the centre of the
   blossom with edible glue and
   thread it up the wire. Secure it
   to the flower centre.

5. Make two more layers of petals
   using the mini blossom and no.
   100 blossom cutters respectively.
   Secure them underneath and in-
   between the first layer of petals.

Bud

6. Make a tiny hook on the end of
   a piece of white wire. Roll a tiny
   teardrop of White SFP, moisten
   the hook with edible glue and
   insert it into the wide end of the
   teardrop.

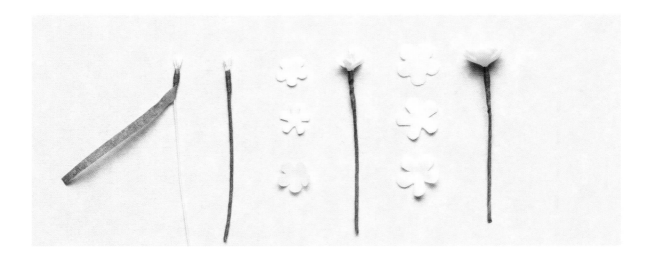

7. Pinch one side of the teardrop to thin the paste. Moisten one side of the flattened paste with edible glue and wrap it around the teardrop to form the bud shape.

Half-open Flower

8. Make the bud, following the method above. Roll out some White SFP and cut out a mini 5-petal blossom. Cut and soften the petals in the same way as before to give the required shape.

9. Moisten the centre with edible glue and secure the petals beneath the bud. Bring up the petals alternately around the bud (i.e. if they were numbered 1 to 5 in a clockwise fashion, start with 1 followed by 3, 5, 2 and 4).

Calyx

10. Colour some White SFP with Leaf Green Paste Food Colour. Roll out the paste and cut out a calyx shape using the mini calyx cutter.

11. Make tiny cuts in each sepal using a craft knife. Place the calyx on a petal pad and soften around the edges using a miniature metal ball tool.

12. Moisten the centre of the calyx with edible glue and thread it up the wire to meet the base of the flower or bud. Add a tiny seedpod by rolling a ball of the green paste and threading it up the wire.

13. Tape the stem with $1/5$-width light green floristry tape.

Colouring

14. Dust the flower centre and stamens with Sunflower Dust Food Colour. Using a flat dusting brush, brush a mixture of Pastel Pink and Cyclamen Dust Food Colours from the edges of the petals towards the centre. Dust the calyx with Holly/Ivy and add a little Edelweiss towards the centre of the calyx.

15. Pass the flower or bud through the steam from a kettle to set the colour.

Leaves

16. Make the leaves in the same way as for the old-fashioned rose (see pages 83 to 84).

WILD ROSE

Materials

Basic materials (see page 6)
SK Professional Dust Food Colours:
Edelweiss, Forest Green, Holly/Ivy,
Sunflower
SK Professional Paste Food Colours:
Leaf Green, Sunflower
SK Sugar Florist Paste (SFP): White

Equipment

Basic tools (see page 6)
Calyx cutter: micro (CEL)
Floristry tape: light green
32-gauge floristry wire: green
33-gauge floristry wire: white
Miniature rose leaf cutters or templates:
medium, small (see page 111)

Miniature stamens: white
Primrose cutters: micro (CEL)

Flower Centre

1. Cut a 33-gauge white floristry wire into eight equal pieces. Cut four miniature stamens in half and tape them to the wire using $^{1}/_{5}$-width white floristry tape. Trim off the excess length from the stamens as you tape down the wire.

2. Colour some White SFP with Sunflower Paste Food Colour to make pale yellow. Roll a 0.5mm diameter ball of paste, brush with edible glue and push it down into the centre of the stamens.

Prick the top of the paste several times using a scriber.

Petals

3. Roll out some White SFP and cut out a primrose flower shape using the cutter. Place the flower shape on a petal pad and soften around the edge using a miniature metal ball tool.

4. Moisten the centre of the flower shape with edible glue and thread it up the wire to meet the stamens.

Calyx

5. Colour some White SFP with Leaf Green Paste Food Colour. Roll out the paste and cut out the calyx shape using the micro cutter. Make tiny cuts on each sepal using fine, pointed scissors or a craft knife.

6. Place the calyx on a petal pad and soften around the edge using a miniature metal ball tool. Moisten the centre with edible glue, thread it up the wire and secure it to the base of the flower.

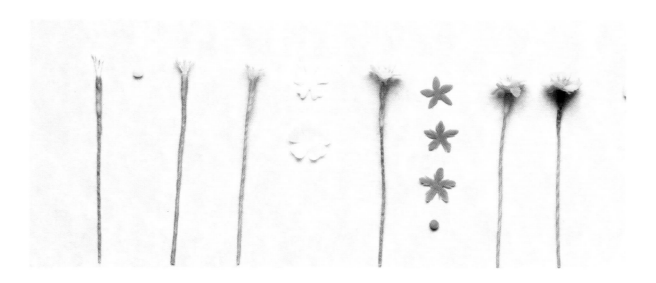

7.   Roll a tiny ball of the green paste and secure it underneath the calyx to represent the seedpod.

8.   Tape down the stem using ⅕-width light green floristry tape.

Colouring

9.   Mix together Sunflower and Edelweiss Dust Food Colours and dust from the edge of the petals towards the centre. Dust the calyx with a mixture of Holly/Ivy and Forest Green Dust Food Colours and brush the edges with the pale yellow colour used on the petals. Dust the flower centre with Sunflower Dust Food Colour.

Buds and Leaves

10.   Make the buds and leaves in the same way as for the rambling rose (see pages 85 to 86).

JASMINE

Materials

Basic materials (see page 6)
SK Professional Dust Food Colours:
Cyclamen, Edelweiss, Forest Green,
Sunflower
SK Professional Paste Food Colour:
Leaf Green
SK Sugar Florist Paste (SFP): White

Equipment

Basic tools (see page 6)
Floristry tape: dark green
35-gauge floristry wire: white
Miniature jasmine leaf cutter or
template (see page 111)
Miniature stamens: white
36SWG scientific wire

Bud

1.   Cut a 35-gauge white floristry wire into eight equal pieces. Roll a tiny ball of White SFP, moisten the end of a piece of wire with edible glue and insert the wire into the paste. Re-shape the paste to make a pointed shape.

Flower

2.   Roll a tiny ball of White SFP into a long teardrop shape. Using a cocktail stick, hollow out the paste from the wide end, then make five cuts in the paste using fine, pointed scissors. Open up the five sections to create the petals.

3. Pinch each of the petals between your thumb and finger, then pinch the end into a point.

4. Insert a 35-gauge white floristry wire down through the top of the flower to form the stem. Pinch the base of the flower to narrow the paste and secure it to the wire.

5. Cut the top off a miniature stamen, brush with edible glue and insert this into the centre of the flower.

Leaves

6. Colour some White SFP with Leaf Green Paste Food Colour. Roll out the paste on a non-stick board, leaving a ridge down the centre. Cut out the leaf shape using the cutter or template.

7. Moisten a scientific wire with edible glue and insert it into the leaf. Place the leaf on a petal pad and mark a central vein from the tip to the base using a cutting wheel. Soften around the edge of the leaf using a miniature metal ball tool, then pinch the leaf from the back to give it a slight curve.

8. Tape down the stem with ¹/₆-width dark green floristry tape.

Colouring

9. Dust the leaves with Forest Green Dust Food Colour and pass through the steam from a kettle to set the colour. Dip into ½-strength confectioners' glaze and allow to dry.

10. Dust the flowers and buds with a mixture of Cyclamen and Edelweiss Dust Food Colours, then dust the base with Forest Green. Pass through steam to set the colour.

Tendrils

11. Tightly twist pieces of ¹/₆-width dark green floristry tape, then wrap them around a scriber to create tiny spirals.

12. Tape the leaves and tendrils together in groups of three or five.

FREESIA

Materials

Basic materials (see page 6)
SK Professional Dust Food Colours:
Holly/Ivy, Lunar Blue, Sunflower
SK Sugar Florist Paste (SFP): White

Equipment

Basic tools (see page 6)
Floristry tape: light green
35-gauge floristry wire: white
Miniature stamens: white

Flower Centre

1. Cut a 35-gauge white floristry into eight equal pieces. Cut three miniature stamens in half, then tape the stamens to the wire using $^1/_5$-width light green floristry tape. Trim off the excess length from the stamens as you tape down the wire.

2. Dust the stamens with Sunflower Dust Food Colour.

Petals

3. Roll a 2mm diameter ball of White SFP into a teardrop shape. Hollow out the teardrop from the wide end using a cocktail stick, then make six cuts in the paste using fine, pointed scissors. Open up the six sections to create the petals.

4. Pinch the sides of each petal to form a point, then flatten each petal between your thumb and finger.

5. Moisten the base of the flower centre with edible glue and pull it down through the flower. Trim off any excess paste at the base of the flower to narrow it down.

Bud

6. Roll a 1mm diameter ball of White SFP and mould it into a teardrop shape. Moisten a 35-gauge white wire with edible glue and insert it into pointed end of the teardrop.

7. Repeat the same method to make more, slightly smaller buds.

Colouring

8. Dust the top of the buds and the edges of the petals with Lunar Blue Dust Food Colour. Dust the base of the larger buds, all of the tiniest buds and the base of the flower with Holly/Ivy Dust Food Colour. Pass through the steam from a kettle to set the colour.

9. Tape the stems together, starting with a tiny bud at the top and increasing the size of the buds down the stem and adding a flower in last. Bend the stem over so that the flowers point upwards.

Assembly

1. Make an 'S' shape flower spray by taping together three old-fashioned roses; two rambling roses and five buds; two wild roses, three buds and six leaves; 3 stems of freesias; and eight rose leaves. Position an old-fashioned rose in the centre, then form the outline of the 'S' shape with two rambling rose buds, joining them behind the central flower. Fill in the spaces along the wires with the other flowers.

2. Decorate the bird cage with the remaining flowers and use a piece of chiffon ribbon to finish off the decoration.

Orchid Duet Wedding Cake

TWO-TIER WEDDING CAKE

Materials

10g (¼oz) apricot glaze
Basic materials (see page 6)
Rich fruit cake ingredients
100g (3½oz) SK Marzipan
200g (7oz) sugarpaste: white
150g (5¼oz) SK Instant Mix Pastillage
100g (3½oz) SK Instant Mix
Professional Royal Icing
SK Professional Paste Food Colours:
Bulrush, Leaf Green
Tracing paper

Equipment

Basic tools (see page 6)
4 flower picks
Food-grade foam sponge
4cm and 6cm (1½" and 2⅜") dome-
shaped cake tins
Piping nozzle: no. 00
7cm, 10cm and 12.5cm (2¾", 4" and 5")
plain round cutters (A)
3mm-width ribbon: light green
5mm-width ribbon: light green

Miniature Flowers and Foliage

9 lady's slipper orchids
9 lemboglossum orchids, 13 buds
9 caladium leaves
13 fern leaves

Cake Boards

1. Mix up the SK Pastillage Instant Mix following the instructions on the pack. Colour the paste with Leaf Green and a touch of Bulrush Paste Food Colours.

2. To make the two cake boards, roll out the pastillage to a thickness of 3mm. Using the cutters, cut out two circles measuring 7cm and 10cm. Make a hole in the centre of the smallest circle using a cocktail stick. Roll out the remaining pastillage to a thickness of 5mm and cut out a 12.5cm circle for the base board. Allow to dry.

3. Mix a little of the pastillage trimmings with cooled, boiled water to make a thick sugar glue. Secure 3mm-width light green ribbon to the edges of the two cake boards and 5mm-width ribbon to the base board using the glue.

Pillar

4. Roll a small piece of white pastillage into a sausage shape. Insert a cocktail stick lengthways through the paste. Roll the paste to form a column and trim away the excess paste from each end, leaving some of the cocktail stick showing at the top and bottom. Allow to dry.

Baking the Cakes

5. Brush the inside of the dome tins with melted butter and coat with sifted flour.

Orchid Duet Wedding Cake Actual Size

6. Mix the cake ingredients together. Spoon the mixture into both tins and level the top.

7. Place the inverted domes into round, heatproof metal cutters to keep them flat and place the cutters and domes onto a baking tray. Bake in a preheated oven at 170°C (Gas Mark 3) for approximately 30 minutes until the cakes are cooked through.

8. Check that the cakes are cooked by inserting a skewer into the centre: when they are baked, it will come out clean. Allow the cakes to cool then carefully remove from the tins using a small palette knife.

9. Brush the surface of the cakes with rum and wrap in aluminium foil. Store at room temperature for a week, brushing occasionally with more rum.

Covering the Cakes

10. Brush the surface of the cakes with apricot glaze. Roll out the marzipan on a non-stick board dusted with icing sugar to a thickness of 3mm. Cover the cakes, smooth the surface with the palm of your hand and trim neatly at the base. Allow to firm overnight.

11. Colour the white sugarpaste with Leaf Green Paste Food Colour and a touch of Bulrush to match the colour of the pastillage boards. Moisten the surface of the cakes with clear alcohol, roll out the sugarpaste to a thickness of 3mm and cover the cakes. Smooth over the surface and trim neatly at the base.

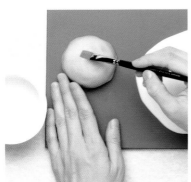

12. Make up the royal icing and place in a piping bag with a no. 00 piping nozzle. Pipe a row of running beads around the base of both cakes.

13. Soften some pastillage with cooled, boiled water to make a strong sugar glue. Use the glue to assemble the pastillage boards, cakes and pillar so that they are held securely in place.

14. Using the same piping nozzle as before, pipe a row of running beads at the top and base of the pillar to disguise the join.

15. Sponge paint the surface of both cakes using royal icing made to soft peak consistency and a small piece of food-grade foam sponge. Allow to dry.

16. Cut a strip of greaseproof paper for each cake measuring the circumference of the cake. Fold each piece in half, in half again, then into thirds to make 12 equal sections. Snip the top into a point, then unfold each strip and carefully secure it around the cake, using a piece of masking tape to secure the ends together. Scratch a pointed line around each cake using a scriber and remove the paper templates.

17. Place some royal icing in a piping bag with a no. 00 nozzle. Pipe a bevelled extension work bridge in a series of scallops, taking care to keep each section the same size. Allow to dry thoroughly. Repeat on both cakes.

18. Pipe vertical drop lines from the template down to the bridge on each cake. Allow to dry.

19. Cut four flower picks in half so that they can be inserted into the cakes (use only the pointed end). Make a small hole in the top tier and three in the base tier for the flower sprays before inserting the flower picks into the cakes. (When using miniature cakes, always make a small hole before inserting a flower pick as the cake can break easily.)

20. Make four miniature flower arrangements and carefully insert the wires into the flower picks.

LADY'S SLIPPER ORCHID

Materials

Basic materials (see page 6)
SK Sugar Florist Paste (SFP): White
SK Professional Dust Food Colours:
Forest Green, Holly/Ivy, Vine
SK Professional Liquid Food Colour:
Holly/Ivy
SK Professional Paste Food Colour:
Leaf Green

Equipment

Basic tools (see page 6)
Floristry tape: light green, white
32-gauge floristry wire: green
35-gauge floristry wire: white
Miniature lady's slipper orchid petal cutters or templates (see page 111)
Miniature lady's slipper orchid leaf cutters or templates (see page 111)
Paintbrush: no. 00000

Column

1. Cut a piece of 35-gauge white wire into eight equal pieces.

2. Roll a tiny ball of White SFP and mould it into a teardrop shape. Moisten the top of a piece of wire with edible glue and insert it into the pointed end of the teardrop.

3. Mould the paste into a 'T' shape using your fingers. Mark a vein down the centre using a craft knife.

4. Dilute a little Holly/Ivy Liquid Food Colour with a little clear alcohol. Using a no. 00000 paintbrush, paint two dots onto the paste and allow to dry. Dust over the top with Vine Dust Food Colour.

Throat

5. Thinly roll out some White SFP and cut out the shape of the throat using the cutter or template.

6. Transfer the throat shape onto a petal pad. Soften the edges and cup each side using a metal ball tool.

7. Brush edible glue along one edge of one side of the throat and bring the other side across. Join the two edges to form the throat shape.

8. Take another piece of 35-gauge white wire, moisten the end with edible glue and work a tiny ball of White SFP down the wire. Brush the paste with edible glue and insert it into the throat. Wrap the base of the throat around the wire.

9. Using a no. 00000 paintbrush and Holly/Ivy Liquid Food Colour diluted with clear alcohol, paint lines down the throat. Allow to dry, then dust with Vine Dust Food Colour.

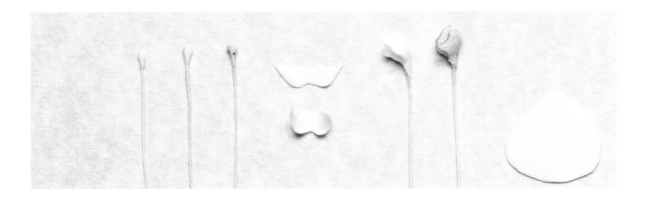

Petals

10. Thinly roll out some White SFP, leaving a ridge down the centre. Using the cutter or template, cut out the top and bottom petal shapes one at a time.

11. Dip the tip of a piece of 35-gauge white floristry wire in edible glue and insert it into the ridge in the paste.

12. Place the petal onto a petal pad and soften the edge with a ball tool. Pinch back the base of the petal on either side and pinch the top to curve it forward slightly.

13. Dilute some Holly/Ivy Liquid Food Colour with clear alcohol and paint lines from the base of the petal on the back and front using a no. 00000 paintbrush.

14. Roll out some White SFP, leaving a ridge down the centre, and cut out the two opposite wing petals using the templates or cutters.

15. Insert a moistened piece of 35-gauge wire into each petal shape. Place each one onto a petal pad and soften the edge.

16. Dilute some Holly/Ivy Liquid Food Colour with clear alcohol. Using a no. 00000 paintbrush, paint lines and dots onto the petals. When dry, dust with Vine Dust Food Colour.

Assembly

17. Using ¼-width light green floristry tape, position the throat underneath the column and tape in place. Add the two side petals followed by the top and bottom petals.

18. Dust the stem with Vine Dust Food Colour. Pass the finished flower through the steam from a kettle to set the colour.

Leaves

19. Cut a 32-gauge green floristry wire into eight equal pieces.

20. Colour some White SFP with a little Leaf Green Paste Food Colour to make a pale green tone. Roll out the paste, leaving a ridge down the centre, and cut out the leaf shape using the cutter or template.

21. Moisten the tip of a piece of wire with edible glue and insert it into the leaf. Pinch the base of the leaf to secure it to the wire and mark a central vein using a cutting wheel.

22. Place the leaf on a petal pad and soften around the edges using a miniature metal ball tool. Turn the leaf over and use the ball tool to mark a line on either side of the centre from the base to the tip.

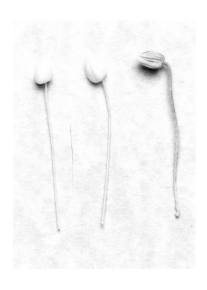

23. Brush the leaf with a mixture of Holly/Ivy and Forest Green Dust Food Colours and pass through the steam from a kettle to set the colour. Allow to dry, then dip into full-strength confectioners' glaze.

Bud

24. Make a tiny hook on the end of a piece of 35-gauge white floristry wire. Roll a ball of White SFP into a teardrop shape, moisten the hook with edible glue and insert it into the wide end of the teardrop.

25. Mark three lines down the teardrop using a cutting wheel. Pinch each of the three sections between your finger and thumb to define the shape.

26. Tape down the stem with ¼-width white floristry tape.

28. Paint lines on the bud using Holly/Ivy Liquid Food Colour and allow to dry. Over-dust the bud and stem with Vine Dust Food Colour.

LEMBOGLOSSUM ORCHID

Materials

Basic materials (see page 6)
SK Professional Dust Food Colours:
Berberis, Edelweiss, Rose, Sunflower
SK Professional Liquid Food Colour:
Rose
SK Sugar Florist Paste (SFP): White

Equipment

Basic tools (see page 6)
Floristry tape: light green
35-gauge floristry wire: white
Silk veining tool (HP)
Miniature lemboglossum orchid
cutters or templates (see page 111)

Column

1. Cut a 35-gauge white floristry wire into eight equal pieces.

2. Roll a tiny ball of White SFP. Moisten the tip of a piece of floristry wire and insert it into the ball of paste. Work the paste down the wire with your fingertips to make a long teardrop shape.

3. Press into the paste from the base to the tip with a metal ball tool to curve the column, then pinch along the back with your fingers to create a ridge.

4. Dilute a little Rose Liquid Food Colour with clear alcohol and paint the inner curve of the column using a no. 00000 paintbrush.

Throat

5. Roll out some White SFP on a non-stick board, leaving a ridge down the centre. Cut out the throat shape using the cutter or template.

6. Moisten the end of a piece of 35-gauge wire with edible glue and insert the wire into the ridge. Frill the edges using a silk veining tool, then pinch a ridge either side of the centre using smooth tweezers.

7. Pinch the top of the throat between your thumb and finger and curl it backwards to give it a natural shape.

8. Dust the base of the throat at the two ridges with Sunflower Dust Food Colour. Dust the rest of the throat with Rose.

Petals

9. Roll out some White SFP on a non-stick board, leaving a ridge down the centre. Cut out the top petal shape using the cutter or template.

10. Moisten the tip of a piece of 35-gauge white floristry wire and insert it into the ridge of the petal. Mark veins on the petal using a craft knife. Pinch the top of the leaf and curl it backwards.

11. Repeat the same method with the two wing petals and leg petals, ensuring you have opposite pairs of each.

12. Dust both sides of the petals in a striped pattern using Berberis and Edelweiss Dust Food Colours. Use diluted Rose Liquid Food Colour and a no. 00000 paintbrush to paint stripes onto the petal.

13. Using ¼-width light green floristry tape, join the column and throat, then add a wing petal on either side. Finally, add the top and leg petals.

Bud

14. Roll a tiny ball of White SFP and insert a moistened 35-gauge white floristry wire into the paste. Mould the ball into a pointed shape and mark three vertical lines down the sides with a craft knife.

15. Dust the buds in a striped pattern and paint lines down the sides in the same way as for the petals.

CALADIUM

Materials

Basic materials (see page 6)
SK Professional Dust Food Colours:
Edelweiss, Fuchsia, Vine
SK Professional Paste Food Colours:
Holly/Ivy, Leaf Green, Sunflower
SK Sugar Florist Paste (SFP): White

Equipment

Basic tools (see page 6)
Floristry tape: moss green
35-gauge floristry wires: white
Food-grade foam sponge (tiny piece)
Leaf bindweed cutter: midi (KB)
Paintbrush: no. 00000

1. Cut a 35-gauge white floristry wire into eight equal pieces.

2. Colour some White SFP with a little Sunflower Paste Food Colour to make a pale yellow tone. Roll out the paste on a non-stick board, leaving a ridge down the centre, and cut out the bindweed shape. Moisten the tip of a piece of wire with edible glue and insert it into the ridge of paste.

3. Place the leaf on a petal pad and soften around the edge with a miniature metal ball tool. Mark veins on the leaf using the pointed end of a Dresden tool.

4. Using a no. 1 paintbrush, dust the front of the leaf with Vine and a mixture of Edelweiss and Fuchsia Dust Food Colours. Dust the back of the leaf with Vine only.

5. Dilute some Leaf Green Paste Food Colour with clear alcohol and paint veins on the leaf using a no. 00000 paintbrush. Allow to dry.

6. Using a tiny piece of sponge, paint the edges of the leaf with diluted Holly/Ivy Paste Food Colour and allow to dry. Pass the leaf through the steam from a kettle to set the dust colour and allow to dry.

7. Tape down the stem with ¼-width moss green floristry tape.

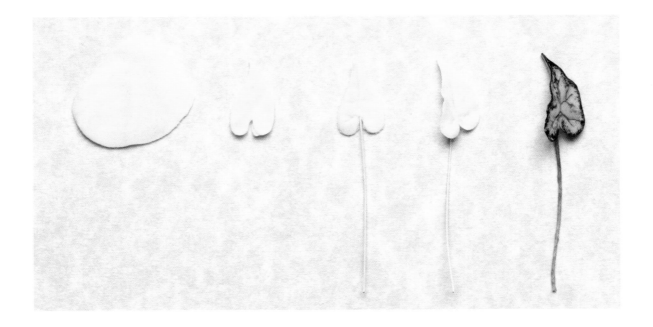

FERN

Materials

Basic materials (see page 6)
SK Professional Designer Dust Food
Colour: Forest Green
SK Professional Paste Food Colour:
Holly/Ivy
SK Sugar Florist Paste (SFP): White

Equipment

Australian fern cutter: small (CCC)
Basic tools (see page 6)
Floristry tape: dark green
35-gauge floristry wires: white
Paintbrush: no. 000

1. Cut a piece of 35-gauge white floristry wire into eight equal pieces.

2. Colour some White SFP with Holly/Ivy Paste Food Colour to make a dark green colour. Roll a tiny ball of paste and push it onto the wire. Work the paste up the wire so that it is the same length as the fern shape.

3. Roll out the remaining dark green-coloured SFP on a non-stick board and cut out the fern shape using the cutter. Mark a vein down the centre and frill around the edge using the pointed end of a Dresden tool.

4. Using a no. 000 paintbrush, apply edible glue down the centre of the leaf and position the paste on the wire down the centre of the leaf. Pinch down the centre from the back with smooth tweezers to secure the wire to the leaf.

5. Dust the leaf with Forest Green Dust Food Colour and pass through the steam from a kettle.

6. Dip the leaf into ½-strength confectioners' glaze and allow to dry.

Assembly

1. To make a round bouquet for the top tier, tape together four lemboglossom orchid buds, keeping the stems fairly long. Add three fern leaves between them and one pointing upwards in the centre. Position three slipper orchids and three lemboglossom orchids in a circle around the central fern leaf, then add three caladium leaves between the fern leaves around the base.

2. Make three triangular-shaped bouquets for the base tier using two slipper orchids, two lemboglossom orchids and two buds, two caladium leaves and three fern leaves. Arrange the flowers in the same way as for the top tier, using the orchids in the centre and the leaves around the base.

3. Cut off the excess wires from each bouquet and insert into a posy pick filled with paste. Carefully insert each posy pick into the wedding cake.

Poppy Fairy

FAIRY

Materials

Basic materials (see page 6)
100g (3½oz) SK Instant Mix Pastillage
50g (1¾oz) SK Instant Mix Royal Icing
SK Leaf Gelatine
100g (3½oz) SK Mexican Modelling
Paste (MMP): White
SK Pollen Style Edible Dust Food
Colour: Pale Green
SK Professional Dust Food Colours:
Berberis, Edelweiss, Holly/Ivy, Pastel
Pink, Poppy, Sunflower
SK Professional Edible Food Paint: White
SK Professional Liquid Food Colours:
Berberis, Bluebell, Bulrush
SK Professional Paste Food Colours:
Holly/Ivy, Sunflower
50g (1¾oz) SK Sugar Florist Paste (SFP):
White

Equipment

Basic tools (see page 6)
6cm and 9cm (2¼" and 3½") circle
cutters
Cling film
Craft dust: apricot
Daisy cutter: no. 109 (TT)
Fairy head mould (HP)
30-gauge floristry wire: gold
Heart-shaped eggcup stand (or similar)
Nail file (new)
Poppy petal templates (see page 111)
2mm-width ribbon: gold
Tissue paper

Miniature Flowers and Foliage

19 poppy flowers (various colours and
stages), 8 buds, 9 leaves

Base

1. Make up the pastillage mix following the instructions on the pack. Colour some of the pastillage with Holly/Ivy Paste Food Colour and some with Sunflower.

2. Roll out the Holly/Ivy-coloured pastillage to a thickness of 2mm and cut out a 9cm circle. Repeat with the Sunflower-coloured pastillage, this time making a 6cm circle. Place both circles on a spare board dusted with cornflour and allow to dry.

3. Smooth any rough edges on the circles using a new nail file. Mix some White SFP with edible glue to make a thick paste and use this to secure gold ribbon around the edge of both circles. Use the paste glue to secure the smaller circle on top of the larger one.

4. Roll out some White SFP and cut out four large petals using the template and a cutting wheel. Place the petals on a petal pad and soften around the edges using a bone tool. Vein and frill each petal by rolling a ceramic silk veining tool from the centre outwards.

5. Lay the petals in pairs opposite each other, with one pair on top of the other. Support the petals with pieces of tissue paper to give them movement and allow to dry.

6. Dust the petals with Poppy Dust Food Colour and pass through the steam from a kettle to set the colour. Place them centrally on the yellow circle and secure in place using the paste glue.

Poppy Fairy Actual Size

Wings

7. To make the wings, place a sheet of gelatine in a bowl and cover with 8 teaspoons of cooled, boiled water.

8. Make the wing shapes using 30-gauge gold floristry wire and twist the ends of the wire together firmly. Place the wire shapes on a piece of cling film.

9. Place the bowl containing the gelatine over a bain-marie and warm the gelatine until it has dissolved. Place half the dissolved gelatine into another bowl and add a few drops of Holly/Ivy Liquid Food Colour. Pour the clear gelatine into the central areas of the wing pieces and the green into the area towards the edges. Allow to dry.

Fairy's Head

10. Colour some White MMP with a hint of Berberis Paste Food Colour to make a flesh tone. Dust the fairy head mould with cornflour, push the paste firmly into the mould and remove.

11. Insert a cocktail stick into the neck and trim off any excess paste at the neck using your fingers. Make the nostrils using a scriber. Allow to dry.

12. When the head is dry, paint the face using liquid food colours and a fine paintbrush. Paint the eyebrows with Bulrush, then paint the whites of the eyes using White Edible Paint. Add Bluebell dots for the pupils, then outline the eyes with Bulrush. Paint the lips using Berberis. Finally, lightly dust the cheeks, chin and forehead with a mixture of Edelweiss, Pastel Pink and Berberis Dust Food Colours.

13. Roll a tiny string of the flesh-coloured MMP and make two pointed ear shapes. Secure these to the sides of the head using edible glue.

Body

14. Colour some White SFP with a little Holly/Ivy Paste Food Colour to make pale green. Roll a 2cm diameter ball of this paste into an oval, then narrow this slightly in the middle to form the waist of the fairy. Make an indent in the shoulders using a ball tool, then pinch the base of the body to form the hips.

15. Make tiny cuts all over the body using fine, pointed scissors. Brush the body with edible glue and cover it with Pale Green Pollen Style Dust Food Colour.

16. Secure the body to the top of the eggcup stand using the strong paste glue made earlier.

17. Colour some White SFP with Sunflower Paste Food Colour, roll out the

paste on a non-stick board and cut out a daisy shape. Lay this over the neck, then secure the head into position, pushing the cocktail stick down through the body.

Legs

18. Roll a 1cm ball of the flesh-coloured MMP, then roll this into a sausage shape. Make a diagonal cut in the centre.

19. Taper the rounded end of each piece, then narrow the paste at the knee and ankle areas by rolling the paste between your fingers. Pinch the paste at the ankles and bend the feet forward. Push into the base of each foot using a bone tool.

20. Secure the legs to the body using paste glue and cross one over the other.

Skirt

21. Roll out some White SFP and cut out four medium poppy petals using the template and a cutting wheel. Soften around the edge of each petal using a bone tool, then vein and frill each petal using a ceramic silk veining tool.

22. Attach the petals around the waist using edible glue and allow to dry. When dry, dust from the edge towards the centre with apricot craft dust.

Arms

23. Roll an 8mm diameter ball of flesh-coloured MMP and make the arms in the same way as the legs. Secure in position using paste glue.

24. Make the sleeves in the same way as the skirt using small petal shapes and secure to the shoulders with edible glue.

Hair

25. Before adding the hair, push the wings into the back of the body and secure in place with paste glue.

26. Make up the royal icing following the instructions on the pack and colour with Bulrush Liquid Food Colour. Place the icing into a piping bag with a no. 1 nozzle and pipe the hair onto the head.

Bouquet

27. Make a hand-tied poppy bouquet and secure this to the fairy's hands.

POPPY

Materials

Basic materials (see page 6)
SK Professional Dust Food Colours:
Holly/Ivy, Marigold, Poppy, Sunflower
SK Professional Pollen Style Dust Food
Colour: Pale Yellow
SK Professional Paste Food Colours:
Holly/Ivy, Sunflower
SK Sugar Florist Paste (SFP): White

Equipment

Basic tools (see page 6)
Poppy petal and leaf cutters: mini and
micro (CEL)
Craft dust: apricot
32-gauge (and 33-gauge, optional)
floristry wire: green
Floristry tape: light green
High-tack craft glue
Miniature stamens: white

Flower Centre

1. Cut a 32- or 33-gauge green
floristry wire into six equal pieces.
Make a tiny hook at the top of a
piece of wire.

2. Colour some White SFP with
Holly/Ivy Paste Food Colour. Roll
a 2mm ball of the green paste
and mould into a teardrop shape.
Moisten the wire hook with
edible glue and insert it into the
pointed end of the teardrop.

3. Using smooth-edged tweezers,
pinch the top of the teardrop
into eight sections. Dust this
top part with Sunflower Dust

Food Colour and the sides with
Holly/Ivy.

Stamens

4. Cut the tops off several
miniature stamens, then cut the
remaining lengths into 5mm
pieces. Pick up the stamens
using tweezers and moisten
the tip of each one with a little
edible glue or high-tack craft
glue. Dip into Pale Yellow Pollen
Style Dust Food Colour. Make
ten stamens in this way for each
poppy.

5. Moisten the bottom of the
stamens with a little high-tack
craft glue and attach them to
the flower centre so that the
tops are level with the top of
the flower centre. Alternatively,
you can lay the stamens onto
a narrow piece of floristry tape
and fold the tape over to hold
them in place before securing
this around the centre.

Petals

6. Colour some White SFP with
Sunflower Paste Food Colour.

Roll out the paste on a non-stick board and cut out a petal shape using the mini poppy petal cutter. Using a craft knife, cut in-between each of the petals to separate them further.

7. Vein the petals using the tip of a ceramic silk veining tool.

8. Moisten the centre of the petals with edible glue and thread the wired flower centre and stamens through it. Secure the petals to the flower centre and arrange the petals to that the smaller ones are inside (on top of) the larger ones.

9. Make more open flowers in the same way and make some with the petals tightly wrapped around the centre.

10. To make half-open flowers, follow the same method using a micro poppy petal cutter. Cut and vein the petals as before, then wrap the petals tightly around the centre.

Bracts

11. To make the bracts for the open and half-open flowers, colour some White SFP with Holly/Ivy Paste Food Colour. Press a small ball of paste flat and snip fine points into the surface on one side using fine, pointed scissors.

12. Make two bracts for each flower and secure them on either side of the flower base.

Bud

13. Make a tiny hook on the end of a 32-gauge piece of green floristry wire. Roll a 3mm ball of the yellow paste into an oval, moisten the hook with edible glue and insert it into one end of the oval.

14. Mark a line down the centre of the oval using a craft knife. Make fine snips all over the paste using fine, pointed scissors.

Leaves

15. Roll out some Holly/Ivy-coloured SFP on a non-stick board, leaving a ridge down the centre. Cut

out a leaf shape using either a mini or micro poppy leaf cutter. Moisten the tip of a piece of 32-gauge green floristry wire with edible glue and insert it into the ridge.

16. Mark veins on the leaf using a plain cutting wheel and the pointed end of a Dresden tool. Soften around the edges of the leaf using a miniature metal ball tool. Pinch the base of the leaf and curve the tip backwards.

Stems

17. Tape the stems of the flowers, buds and leaves with $1/5$-width light green floristry tape.

Colouring

18. Dust the bracts, buds and leaves with Holly/Ivy Dust Food Colour. Dust the central area of the petals with Holly/Ivy Dust Food Colour. Dust the main part of the petals with Sunflower Dust Food Colour, then brush the edges with Poppy, Marigold, Sunflower or apricot.

19. Pass all the leaves, buds and flowers through the steam from a kettle to set the colour.

Assembly

Tape the flowers into a small bouquet for the fairy to hold and place it in position.

TEMPLATES

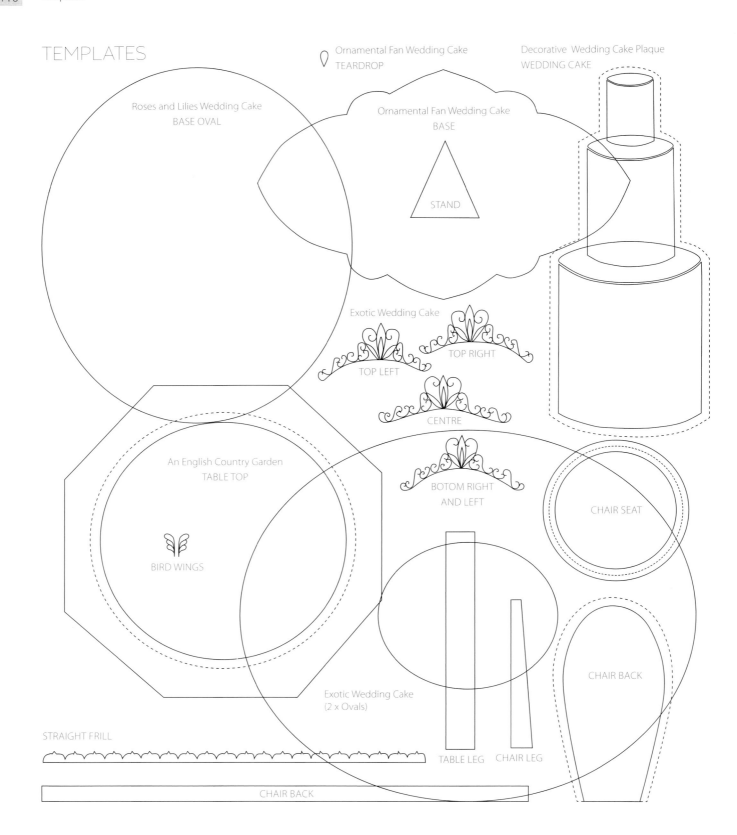

Ornamental Fan Wedding Cake
TEARDROP

Decorative Wedding Cake Plaque
WEDDING CAKE

Roses and Lilies Wedding Cake
BASE OVAL

Ornamental Fan Wedding Cake
BASE

STAND

Exotic Wedding Cake

TOP LEFT

TOP RIGHT

CENTRE

An English Country Garden
TABLE TOP

BOTOM RIGHT
AND LEFT

CHAIR SEAT

BIRD WINGS

CHAIR BACK

Exotic Wedding Cake
(2 x Ovals)

STRAIGHT FRILL

TABLE LEG   CHAIR LEG

CHAIR BACK

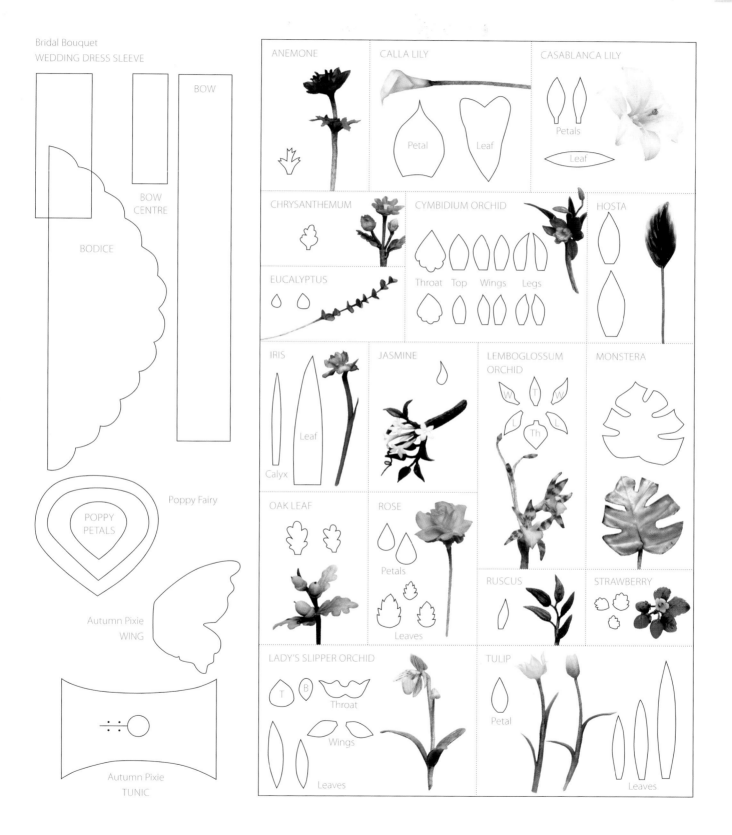

Bridal Bouquet
WEDDING DRESS SLEEVE

BOW

BOW CENTRE

BODICE

Poppy Fairy

POPPY PETALS

Autumn Pixie
WING

Autumn Pixie
TUNIC

ANEMONE

CALLA LILY

Petal

Leaf

CASABLANCA LILY

Petals

Leaf

CHRYSANTHEMUM

CYMBIDIUM ORCHID

Throat   Top   Wings   Legs

HOSTA

EUCALYPTUS

IRIS

Leaf

Calyx

JASMINE

LEMBOGLOSSUM ORCHID

W   T   W

L   Th   L

MONSTERA

OAK LEAF

ROSE

Petals

Leaves

RUSCUS

STRAWBERRY

LADY'S SLIPPER ORCHID

T   B

Throat

Wings

Leaves

TULIP

Petal

Leaves

SUPPLIERS

Shops

A Piece of Cake
18-20 Upper High Street
Thame
Oxon
OX9 3EX
UK
Tel: 01844 213428
Email: sales@sugaricing.com
Website: www.apieceofcakethame.co.uk

Confectionery Supplies
Unit 11a, b and c
Foley Trading Estate
Hereford
HR1 2SF
UK
Tel: 01432 371451/029 2037 2161
      (mail order)
Email: kclements@btinternet.com
Website: www.confectionerysupplies.co.uk

Jane Asher Party Cakes and Tearoom
22-24 Cale Street
London
SW3 3QU
UK
Tel: 020 7584 6177
Email: info@janeasher.com
Website: www.janeasher.com

Squires Kitchen Sugarcraft
Squires House
3 Waverley Lane
Farnham
Surrey
GU9 8BB
UK
Tel: 0845 22 55 67 1/2 (from UK)
      +44 (0)1252 711749 (from overseas)
Email: info@squires-group.co.uk
Online shop: www.squires-shop.com
Website: www.squires-group.co.uk

Tårtdecor
Bulygatan 14
442 40 KUNGÄLV
Sweden
Tel: +46 303 514 70
Email: info@tartdecor.se
Website: www.tartdecor.se

Distributors

Culpitt Ltd.
Jubilee Industrial Estate
Ashington
Northumberland
NE63 8UQ
UK
Tel: 01670 814545
Email: info@culpitt.com
Website: www.culpitt.com

Guy, Paul & Co. Ltd.
Unit 10, The Business Centre
Corinium Industrial Estate
Raans Road
Amersham
Buckinghamshire
HP6 6FB
UK
Tel: 01494 432121
Email: sales@guypaul.co.uk
Website: www.guypaul.co.uk

Renshaw
Crown Street
Liverpool
L8 7RF
UK
Email: enquiries@renshaw-nbf.co.uk
Website: www.renshaw-nbf.co.uk

Squires Kitchen
Website: www.squires-group.co.uk

Manufacturer Abbreviations

Ateco cutters (A)
See Guy, Paul & Co.

CelCakes & CelCrafts (CEL)
Tools and equipment available from your local sugarcraft supplier.

Clean Cut Cutters (CCC)
See A Piece of Cake.

Coronet Porcelain Ltd. (CP)
Cutters, veiners and cold porcelain available from your local sugarcraft supplier.

Fine Cut Sugarcraft (FC)
Cutters available from your local sugarcraft supplier.

Holly Products (HP)
Tools and moulds available from your local sugarcraft supplier.

Jem Cutters CC (JEM)
Cutters available from your local sugarcraft supplier.

Kit Box (KB)
Tools, cutters and equipment available from your local sugarcraft supplier.

Squires Kitchen (SK)
Edibles, tools, veiners and publications available from Squires Kitchen Sugarcraft and your local sugarcraft supplier.

Tinkertech Two cutters (TT)
See Confectionery Supplies

Wilton (W)
Edibles and decorations available from your local sugarcraft supplier.